ESSAYS:
THREE DEGREES

Denver C. Snuffer, Jr.

Published in the United States by Mill Creek Press.
Mill Creek Press is a registered trademark of Mill Creek Press, LLC.
www.millcreekpress.com

ISBN-10: 0989150356
ISBN-13: 978-0-9891503-5-4

Printed in the United States of America on acid-free paper.

First Edition

Cover design by CreateSpace.

CONTENTS

PREFACE

I have made drafts of these essays available through my blog but always intended to update and put them into print.

The version here is slightly modified from what is available on the blog. The greatest difference is in the *Elijah* essay where several footnotes have been added and a number of needed corrections and amplifications have been made.

I appreciate the contributions that have been made to help with this work, including those of Mill Creek Press, who allows me total editorial control over the content of what I write. This makes me alone accountable for the content, and therefore any errors are my own.

These essays are offered in the hope of advancing understanding of the Mormon faith which I believe. The faith is vast, and our comprehension of it is incomplete and inadequate. Hopefully these essays will help stir others to think more deeply about this marvelous, wonderful[1] gift restored through Joseph Smith.

---

[1]   See Isa. 29:14.

This is the fourteenth volume I have written. These essays expand topics introduced in earlier books. Although these are "stand alone" essays, a reader will benefit most if they are acquainted with what I have written previously.

These three essays are taken from three talks. The topics correspond to three levels of Mormon cosmology. The first essay begins with pre-earth, and discusses Celestial events. It was originally given to a small group of invited guests in my home. The second involves the connection between earth and heaven forged through a Terrestrial holiness in which Christ and man are able to interact. This talk was delivered in public to a group acquainted with my writings at a location in Spanish Fork, Utah. The third involves Telestial or worldly concerns with Mormon history. This talk was originally delivered at the Sunstone Symposium in Salt Lake City, an event for Mormon intellectuals. The topics and venues both reflect these symbolic levels. Hence the title of this volume: *Essays: Three Degrees*. The order was set to descend, rather than ascend, because that is where we find ourselves and Mormonism.

Holiness is for us, as for all of Adam's descendants, merely aspirational and elusive. When we acquire it, we always find it is derivative through Christ, and not original with us. Hopefully this volume will stimulate your aspirations.

Denver C. Snuffer, Jr.
Sandy, Utah
June 21, 2014

ESSAY 1:
FIRST THREE WORDS

FIRST THREE WORDS

AN ESSAY ABOUT THE FIRST THREE WORDS
SPOKEN BY PLAYERS IN THE ENDOWMENT

Brothers and sisters, as you sit here, you will hear the voices of three persons who represent Elohim, Jehovah and Michael . . .

ELOHIM: Jehovah, Michael: see . . .

A great deal is contained in these first three spoken words from the Endowment. This essay represents my current thinking on the material, I could not have written this ten years ago. Nor do I expect that ten years from now I would write this same essay. My understanding changes over time, and this is a snapshot of my understanding taken from a moving picture. I hope it is useful to you.

This essay is all about the first three words spoken in the presentation of the Endowment. Keep that in mind. As we begin there are foundational materials which may seem unrelated at first. Bear with it, because we are only speaking about one subject, and everything will tie back to that single subject.

I should clarify at the start this subject is not off limits or inappropriate to discuss. Nor is this essay something that violates any covenant. None of the keys, signs, tokens, names or sacred information guarded by covenants and obligations to keep as secret are discussed in this essay. Therefore, a faithful Latter-day Saint reader should not have any apprehension about inappropriate disregard for obligations to keep the sacred from public disclosure as you read this essay. I agree with Hugh Nibley's assessment that the greatest protection for the mysteries is the general disinterest of people. However, I do not rely upon such disinterest to protect mysteries which we share in sacred places. I police what I discuss, with the covenants I have made always in mind.[2]

An 11th century Muslim scholar attributed this saying to Christ: "He who bestows knowledge on the ignorant wastes it, and he who withholds it from the worthy has done them wrong."[3] This requires balance. If I err in this essay, I hope to avoid doing wrong to the worthy.

I am convinced all truth should fit within the framework of existing scripture. Anything new that contradicts established scripture ought to be rejected. However, this does not mean there are no unfamiliar truths to be discovered merely because you are familiar with all existing scripture. Indeed, just because you have never seen it before does not mean new truth should be rejected when it is brought to your attention. One of mankind's great defects has always been resistance to new truth. Joseph lamented the Saints' resistance to being taught: *I have tried for a number of years to get the minds of the Saints prepared to receive the things of God; but*

---

[2] Although I was excommunicated in September, 2013, I have always kept the Temple covenants, and have no intention of violating them in the future.

[3] Al-Ghazali, reference found in *The Niche of Lights*, p. 2.

we frequently see some of them, after suffering all they have for the work of God, will fly to pieces like glass as soon as anything comes that is contrary to their traditions: they cannot stand the fire at all. How many will be able to abide a celestial law, and go through and receive their exaltation, I am unable to say, as many are called, but few are chosen." (*TPJS*, 331.) Christ had the same problem with the Nephites. He lamented their woeful inability to take in what He had been commanded to teach them: "I perceive that ye are weak, that ye cannot understand all my words which I am commanded of the Father to speak unto you at this time. Therefore, go ye unto your homes, and ponder upon the things which I have said, and ask of the Father, in my name, that ye may understand, and prepare your minds for the morrow, and I come unto you again." (3 Ne. 17:2-3.) We tend to fear learning anything new. That is a curious defect found only in adults.

Joseph explained his role (as is true of any prophet) included the obligation to teach forgotten truths. They became "new" truths because the current generation allowed the truth to be forgotten. As Joseph put it: *"It has always been my province to dig up hidden mysteries new things for my hearers."* (*TPJS*, 364.) It is surely true the testimony of Jesus IS the spirit of prophecy. (Rev. 19:10.) And it is equally true that without the testimony of prophets we forfeit truth by the corrosive environment of this Telestial Kingdom where we all live.[4]

Joseph once explained that truth could be "tasted" when it is taught. As he put it: *"This is good doctrine. It tastes good. I can*

---

[4] Prophets have received the Holy Ghost, and therefore are able to understand the true meaning of scripture. They do not rely on the tools of the scholar, which produce different and inaccurate interpretations of scripture. Instead, they are in possession of the same Spirit as the original authors, and therefore know what was in the mind of the writer when the scriptures were written. See JS-H 1:73-74.

*taste the principles of eternal life, and so can you. They are given
to me by the revelations of Jesus Christ; and I know that when I
tell you these words of eternal life as they are given to me, you
taste them, and I know that you believe them. You say honey is
sweet, and so do I. I can also taste the spirit of eternal life. I know
it is good; and when I tell you of these things which were given
me by inspiration of the Holy Spirit, you are bound to receive
them as sweet, and rejoice more and more." (TPJS, 355.)*

As an aside, the compilation found in the *Teachings of the
Prophet Joseph Smith* was prepared by Joseph Fielding Smith
based on the original notes of those who heard Joseph's talks.
Those original notes from the Nauvoo era talks given by Joseph
which Joseph Fielding Smith used to compile the *TPJS* have been
gathered into the book *The Words of Joseph Smith: The Contemporary Accounts of the Nauvoo Discourses of the Prophet Joseph*,
compiled and edited by Andrew F. Ehat and Lyndon W. Cook. The
quote above is an amalgamation of the notes of *Wilford Woodruff's Journal*, appearing on page 364 of *WJS*: "this is good doctrin, it taste good, I can taste the principles of eternal life, so can
you, they are given to me by the revelations of Jesus Christ and I
know you believe it." The *Thomas Bullock Report* appears at page
352: "you say honey is Sweet & so do I. I can also taste the Sp of
Eternal life I know it is good & when I tell you of these things that
were given me by Insp of the H S. you are bound to rece it as sweet
& I rej more & more." The *William Clayton Report* is on page 360:
"I know that when I tell you those words of eternal life that are
given to me I know you taste it and I know you believe it."

A little farther into this we will carefully consider the original
notes from two of Joseph's final talks. These notes are our most
accurate source for his actual words, and words matter a great deal.

Because we will be discussing some of Joseph's most lofty teachings, we will rely upon the original notes, and not the *TPJS*.

Joseph used "taste" and Nephi used "feel" to describe the very intangible way we detect truth as it is presented to us. Nephi, when talking to his older brothers about how to know a matter is true, used these words: "Ye are swift to do iniquity but slow to remember the Lord your God. Ye have seen an angel, and he spake unto you; yea, ye have heard his voice from time to time; and he hath spoken unto you in a still small voice, but ye were past feeling, that ye could not feel his words;" (1 Ne. 17:45.) This is delicate, refined and subtle. It is intended to stretch us, to quiet us down and calm our minds. We are supposed to receive our own anecdotal evidence which is personal to us, adapted to our own capacities, and something sufficient to convince us it comes from God. It is *always* the case that these experiences are going to be anecdotal. Only the prepared are going to experience them. Others are excluded. One of the best examples of how this works is found in Daniel:

And in the four and twentieth day of the first month, as I was by the side of the great river, which is Hiddekel; Then I lifted up mine eyes, and looked, and behold a certain man clothed in linen, whose loins were girded with fine gold of Uphaz: His body also was like the beryl, and his face as the appearance of lightning, and his eyes as lamps of fire, and his arms and his feet like in colour to polished brass, and the voice of his words like the voice of a multitude. And *I Daniel alone saw the vision: for the men that were with me saw not the vision*; but a great quaking fell upon them, so that they fled to hide themselves. Therefore *I was left alone, and saw this great vision*, and there remained no strength in me: for my comeliness was turned in me into corruption, and I retained no strength. Yet heard I the voice of his words: and when I heard the voice of his words, then was I in a deep sleep on my face, and my face toward the ground. (Daniel 10: 4-9, emphasis added.)

Daniel's experience was real. But it was not open to the view of the unworthy. The physically demanding nature of this kind of experience is often referred to in scripture. Joseph Smith went through it when he collapsed, exhausted and returning home after the night spent with Moroni. (See JS-H 1:48.) Also, King Lamoni, his wife and all within his house had a similar reaction to his great revelation. (See Alma 18:40-19:30.) Every such experience is real. They are physical and exhausting. But they are also necessarily personal and cannot be shared. Those lacking faith to have such access are free to disbelieve in them. It is true that this kind of "oil" cannot be shared. (See Matt. 25:8-9.)

Taste and feel are two ways to communicate the highly personal nature of such experiences. I can think of two analogies using the idea of "balance" to illustrate the same point: When you ski, there is a 'fall line' on any given slope where the route you take down the mountain cooperates with the terrain, gravity and balance. You can feel the 'fall line' when you are in it. There is such harmony between the skier and the slope that everything goes into balance. You know it is right. You can sense the balance, the harmony when you are in the fall line. It becomes effortless.

The other comes from riding a Harley Davidson. There is a curious perfection about the Harley big-twins. The center of gravity is located below the axle and almost dead center between them. This low and middle center of gravity makes for harmony between rider and machine as soon as it is put into motion. Despite the great weight of the bike, when it is in motion, even at slow speeds, it is nimble. Riding on a Harley you can feel this nimble, stable balance. It is so delicate a matter that you can sense the difference between posted speed limit on the road and the design speed of the engineer who designed the roadway. It can be described with words, but the balance must be experienced to actually know what those words are trying to convey.

In both the skiing example and the Harley, the harmony in the movement with the skis or the motorcycle results in a oneness. Everything is an extension of your own body, and you can feel yourself in harmony with the terrain over which you are moving. These are childlike experiences. They force you into the moment. They put you into the *now* and all else is removed. You are compelled to 'take no thought for the morrow' because the moment overwhelms the senses.

You probably have your own experiences you could use to illustrate the point. Whether it is "taste" or "feel" or "balance" or some other highly subjective experience; the point is that you can know from this experience when it is just right. This is what hearing a new truth should be like. You were meant to know the truth. You long for it. We all do. There is something inside us that cannot be satisfied until we are back in contact with it. This is what is delicious about the Gospel. This is what we should be able to feast upon as a result of being a Latter-day Saint. The scriptures and Joseph's teachings are filled with this idea. When we turn the Gospel into something stale and uninviting, we are profaning the great joy, the great light the Gospel was intended to convey. [I've written a chapter on Joy in *Eighteen Verses* that demonstrates this idea.]

Every person who joins the church is expected to do so because of Moroni 10:4: "And when ye shall receive these things, I would exhort you that ye would ask God, the Eternal Father, in the name of Christ, if these things are not true; and if ye shall ask with a sincere heart, with real intent, having faith in Christ, he will manifest the truth of it unto you, by the power of the Holy Ghost." Missionaries teach people that God will speak to them. Investigators are assured this promise was meant for them. Then when the exciting experience of finding that God will actually speak to them results in an answer to prayer, a new life begins. That new life is accompanied by baptism and laying on of hands for the gift of the Holy Ghost. All of it is exciting, filling the senses and bringing the convert back into contact with God.

I went through the process when I was 19 years old. I learned for myself that God would answer prayer in this day, just as had been the case in the scriptures. Therefore, I joined the church. After 4 years as a member of the church, I began law school. By the time I finished law school, I was seven years into membership. When I graduated from law school, I was troubled by the thought there was nothing more to learn. That apprehension was because of the limited information being taught by the institutional church. The church, of course, has an obligation to new converts to teach fundamental doctrines. The church does not and cannot address the kind of learning that is required to continue throughout your life. (I address this in *The Second Comforter: Conversing With the Lord Through the Veil*.)

As a result, I realized I could not depend upon the church's established curriculum and must continue the search on my own. The search has continued apace. I thank some of you for your contributions, both directly and indirectly to my continuing education. I remain an ignorant man, but still an eager student. Moses reported this statement from the Lord, in Chapter 1:5: "Wherefore, no man can behold all my works, except he behold all my glory; and no man can behold all my glory, and afterwards remain in the flesh on the earth." So there are absolute limits on learning. But there is nevertheless a great deal of knowledge which can and should be gained here. The scriptures also tell us we can know "all truth." (Moroni 10:5, see also D&C 50:24 and 93:28.) [Those promises should be read in the context of what mortals living here are permitted to know. It is a great deal. Nevertheless, there will always be some few questions we are not allowed to have answered while mortal.]

Before I speak, I need to know what I have to say is first approved by heaven. I take as an absolute standard the statement in D&C 42:14: "if ye receive not the Spirit ye shall not teach." Therefore, when I teach it will only be with permission and following the direction of a higher source. I also believe the Lord's warning found in JST Matt 12:31: "And again I say unto you, That every idle word that men shall speak, they shall give account thereof in the day of judgment." So I expect to be accountable and to be judged for the words I speak this evening.

The Apostle Paul

The Apostle Paul warned about our day. We are in the middle of the problem right now. His warning is found in 2 Timothy:

1 This know also, that in the last days perilous times shall come.

2 For men shall be lovers of their own selves, covetous, boasters, proud, blasphemers, disobedient to parents, unthankful, unholy,

3 Without natural affection, trucebreakers, false accusers, incontinent, fierce, despisers of those that are good,

4 Traitors, **heady, high minded**, lovers of pleasures more than lovers of God;

5 **Having a form of godliness, but denying the power thereof:** from such turn away.

6 For of this sort are they which creep into houses, and lead captive silly women laden with sins, led away with divers lusts,

7 **Ever learning, and never able to come to the knowledge of the truth.**

2 Timothy 3:1-7

This is a troubling problem to consider. I listen to talks on KBYU given at Education Week, or General Conferences, or Forum talks at BYU, BYU-Idaho or BYU-Hawaii, or the Women's Conferences. Some speakers give talks just as they should—using the Spirit as a guide and speaking words of eternal life. Others, however, take their educational background as their guide. Whether they are trained in economics, education, business, philosophy, law or some other discipline, what they teach are the principles they learned in their specialty. They presume their education is so "true" that they are justified in relying upon it. And so they teach with their own learning, mingling it with scriptures, and selling us the philosophies of men. Such teachers lack any power of godliness, merely pretending to have the form. (See 2 Ne. Chapter 28.) I hope in everything I say or write to avoid being heady or high-minded. But as soon as a person thinks they are safe from error, they are likely to be fooled. I need your prayers and faith to help us get only the truth here tonight. We cannot rely only on a form of godliness, but must seek the actual power of godliness. It is by relying upon the Spirit alone which can let us come to the knowledge of the truth. Because I am speaking to a small group here in my home, I do not expect this talk to be anything other than an intimate discussion among carefully chosen friends. In such a gathering, I hope the Spirit will allow inspiration, where more can be taught and even the speaker is able to learn. President Marion Romney once remarked that he knew when he was teaching by the Spirit because he would learn something new.

Joseph Smith

In the revelation found in D&C 88:118, it was revealed through Joseph that: "And as **all have not faith**, seek ye diligently and teach one another words of wisdom; yea, seek ye out of the best books words of wisdom; seek learning, even by study and also by faith." This revelation gives the preference to learning by "faith" and only secondarily, as a consequence of the failure of faith, to learn by using "the best books" and "study." I study relentlessly. But I trust only the Spirit to guide me when accepting new truth. As a result, I reject many things I hear on KBYU, in church or in Deseret Book publications.

Nephi

Nephi also warned us about the limits of education in our day. We read in 2 Ne 9:28-29: "O that cunning plan of the evil one! O the vainness, and the frailties, and the foolishness of men! When they are learned they think they are wise, and they hearken not unto the counsel of God, for they set it aside, supposing they know of themselves, wherefore, their wisdom is foolishness and it profiteth them not. And they shall perish. But to be learned is good if they hearken unto the counsels of God." Learning must be subordinated to the "counsels of God" if it is to be of use in saving our souls. Otherwise we rely upon "foolishness" while calling it "wisdom."

Moroni

Moroni gave us the formula for knowing all truth in Moroni 10:4-5: "And by the power of the Holy Ghost ye may know the truth of all things." [I have devoted a chapter in *Eighteen Verses* to this verse.] This was the formula we were to follow. Find truth using the Spirit. Rely upon that source. It will lead you to know the "fullness" of all truth.

We read in D&C 93:1: "Verily, thus saith the Lord: It shall come to pass that every soul who forsaketh his sins and cometh unto me, and calleth on my name, and obeyeth my voice, and keepeth my commandments, shall see my face and know that I am[.]" This is the final truth. For this is the definition of eternal life: "And this is life eternal, that they might know thee the only true God, and Jesus Christ, whom thou hast sent." (John 17:3.)

I referred above to 2 Nephi 28. That is an important enough warning that it bears setting out at length here. I have interrupted the flow of the chapter below to identify the ten times he warns us in this single chapter how in the last days we will fail, be misled and accept as true things which are false. Below the warnings are highlighted in bold capital letters:

2 Nephi 28

> 3 For it shall come to pass in that day that the churches which are built up, and not unto the Lord, when the one shall say unto the other: Behold, I, I am the Lord's; and the others shall say: I, I am the Lord's; and thus shall every one say that hath built up churches, and not unto the Lord

> 4 And they shall contend one with another; and their priests shall contend one with another, and they shall teach with their learning, and deny the Holy Ghost, which giveth utterance. **FIRST WARNING!**

5 And they deny the power of God, the Holy One of Israel; **SECOND WARNING!** and they say unto the people: Hearken unto us, and hear ye our precept; **THIRD WARNING!** for behold there is no God today, for the Lord and the Redeemer hath done his work, and he hath given his power unto men;

6 Behold, hearken ye unto my precept; **FOURTH WARNING!** if they shall say there is a miracle wrought by the hand of the Lord, believe it not; for this day he is not a God of miracles; he hath done his work.

11 Yea, they have all gone out of the way; they have become corrupted.

12 Because of pride, and because of false teachers, and false doctrine, **FIFTH WARNING!** their churches have become corrupted, and their churches are lifted up; because of pride they are puffed up.

13 They rob the poor because of their fine sanctuaries; they rob the poor because of their fine clothing; and they persecute the meek and the poor in heart, because in their pride they are puffed up.

14 They wear stiff necks and high heads; yea, and because of pride, and wickedness, and abominations, and whoredoms, they have all gone astray save it be a _few, who are the humble followers of Christ_; nevertheless, they are led, that in many instances they do err because they are taught by the precepts of men. **SIXTH WARNING!**[5]

15 O the wise, and the learned, and the rich, that are puffed up in the pride of their hearts, and all those who preach false doctrines, **SEVENTH WARNING!** and all those

---

[5]   As an aside, I put the underlined and italicized excerpt from this verse into the dedication of my first book, *The Second Comforter*. That was quite deliberate. I think Nephi tells us in the verse exactly what we are faced with in this dispensation. That, however, is a whole separate subject.

who commit whoredoms, and pervert the right way of the Lord, wo, wo, wo be unto them, saith the Lord God Almighty, for they shall be thrust down to hell!

16 Wo unto them that turn aside the just for a thing of naught and revile against that which is good, and say that it is of no worth! For the day shall come that the Lord God will speedily visit the inhabitants of the earth; and in that day that they are fully ripe in iniquity they shall perish.

17 But behold, if the inhabitants of the earth shall repent of their wickedness and abominations they shall not be destroyed, saith the Lord of Hosts.

18 But behold, that great and abominable church, the whore of all the earth, must tumble to the earth, and great must be the fall thereof.

19 For the kingdom of the devil must shake, and they which belong to it must needs be stirred up unto repentance, or the devil will grasp them with his everlasting chains, and they be stirred up to anger, and perish;

20 For behold, at that day shall he rage in the hearts of the children of men, and stir them up to anger against that which is good.

21 And others will he pacify, and lull them away into carnal security, that they will say: All is well in Zion;[6] yea, Zion prospereth, all is well and thus the devil cheateth their souls, and leadeth them away carefully down to hell.

22 And behold, others he flattereth away, and telleth them there is no hell; and he saith unto them: I am no devil, for there is noneand thus he whispereth in their ears, until he grasps them with his awful chains, from whence there is no deliverance.

---

[6]   The term "Zion" is never used to describe Gentiles who are unacquainted with the Gospel. It therefore necessarily refers to Latter-day Saints.

23 Yea, they are grasped with death, and hell; and death, and hell, and the devil, and all that have been seized therewith must stand before the throne of God, and be judged according to their works, from whence they must go into the place prepared for them, even a lake of fire and brimstone, which is endless torment.

24 Therefore, wo be unto him that is at ease in Zion!

25 Wo be unto him that crieth: All is well!

26 Yea, wo be unto him that hearkeneth unto the precepts of men, and denieth the power of God, and the gift of the Holy Ghost! **EIGHTH WARNING!**

27 Yea, wo be unto him that saith: We have received, and we need no more!

28 And in fine, wo unto all those who tremble, and are angry because of the truth of God! For behold, he that is built upon the rock receiveth it with gladness; and he that is built upon a sandy foundation trembleth lest he shall fall.

29 Wo be unto him that shall say: We have received the word of God, and we need no more of the word of God, for we have enough! **NINTH WARNING!**

30 For behold, thus saith the Lord God: I will give unto the children of men line upon line, precept upon precept, here a little and there a little; and blessed are those who hearken unto my precepts, and lend an ear unto my counsel, for they shall learn wisdom; for unto him that receiveth I will give more; and from them that shall say, We have enough, from them shall be taken away even that which they have. [This is an ominous warning that Alma will revisit in Alma 12:10-13. This verse inspired the teaching found there. They should be read together.]

31 Cursed is he that putteth his trust in man, or maketh flesh his arm, or shall hearken unto the precepts of men,

save their precepts shall be given by the power of the Holy Ghost. **TENTH WARNING!**

32 Wo be unto the Gentiles, saith the Lord God of Hosts! For notwithstanding I shall lengthen out mine arm unto them from day to day, they will deny me; nevertheless, I will be merciful unto them, saith the Lord God, if they will repent and come unto me; for mine arm is lengthened out all the day long, saith the Lord God of Hosts.

Remember that Nephi is giving us his "valedictory" address here. It is his final, great summation of all he has tried to teach. He concluded his record with these sober warnings. It is astonishing to me we have this lesson and yet give so little notice to it. He is warning us to avoid the wisdom of men, the arm of flesh, or in other words the social sciences, as a basis for decision-making. Nephi is telling us that the institutions of education, all our higher learning, is NOT to be the final source of truth for us. For us the Holy Ghost alone is to be the final guide.

Moroni 10:5 is Moroni's valedictory warning to us at the end of the entire Nephite civilization. He gives us the same message: "And by the power of the Holy Ghost ye may know the truth of all things." We are supposed to receive truth only from the Holy Ghost. If there is no witness to you from the Holy Ghost, then there is no truth being taught you.

I found a talk given in General Conference by Elder Theodore M. Burton that is so relevant to the point I decided to quote it at length. It can be found in *Conference Report*, April 1961, Afternoon Meeting, at pages 128-129:

A little learning is a dangerous thing, and too many men and too many women who have become experts in a tiny field of learning think that because they are trained in that field of learning, they are experts in all fields of learning.

Many men who are well-trained in one limited field feel that this equally qualifies them to express learned opinions in the field of faith and religion, although many of them have never done any studying nor taken a class in these subjects. So, I say that the problem is not that they know too much, but that they know too much of what just isn't so. Actually they know too little. They have closed their minds to anything except the philosophies of men.

Now, brothers and sisters, in our Church in this day and age, when education is becoming more and more popular and more and more necessary, there is grave danger of intellectual apostasy. The problem is that of a closed mind as I see it. Jacob taught this beautifully as we read it in the Book of Mormon. "O that cunning plan of the evil one! O the vainness, and the frailties, and the foolishness of men! When they are learned they think they are wise, and they hearken not unto the counsel of God, for they set it aside, supposing they know of themselves, wherefore their wisdom is foolishness and it profiteth them not. And they shall perish. But to be learned is good if they hearken unto the counsels of God." (2 Nephi 9:28-29.) That we should emphasize, "To be learned is good."

What causes intellectual apostasy? Why do some learned men and women turn from the faith? It is not learning for there are hundreds of us, thousands of us, equally well-trained. It isn't being exposed to different ideas, for we too were exposed to these ideas in the finest universities of the land. Why then, do they lose their testimony? Principally out of vanity and pride. They want to impress others with their learning. To put it indelicately, it is the problem of the swelled head, because that is exactly what the Prophet said. ". . . whoso knocketh," Jacob said, "to him will he open, and the wise, and the learned, and they who are rich, who are puffed up" and that you see is just exactly what he said "who are puffed up because of their learning, and their wisdom, and their riches yea, they are they whom he despiseth; and save they shall cast these things away, and consider themselves fools before God, and come down in the depths of humility, he will not open unto them." (Ibid., 9:42.)

Now remember, it isn't the simplicity of the tool that determines its value but the skill of the workman who uses that tool. God, I am sure, would prefer to use the most skilled, the most able, the best trained person that he could find, but that person must be humble and he must be teachable, and he must be willing to learn something new. We, with all our learning, stand just at the threshold of things that we need to know, just at the beginning of wisdom, with the rudiments of wisdom in our hands. As Paul taught, the workman is more important than the tool. "For ye see your calling, brethren," he said, "how that not many wise men after the flesh, not many mighty, not many noble, are called: But . . . God hath chosen the weak things of the world to confound the things which are mighty; . . . that no flesh should glory in his presence. But of him are ye in Christ Jesus who of God is made unto us wisdom, and righteousness, and sanctification and redemption." (1 Cor. 1:26–27, 29–30.)

Over the library of the Utah State University stands in big gold letters a statement taken from the scriptures: "Get wisdom, and with all thy getting get understanding." (Prov. 4:7) We must feed the spirit as well as the mind and as well as the body. I plead with our youth, get learning, and with all your getting get understanding. Get learning of the spirit. Get learning of the mind. Get learning of the soul, and become a rounded man or a rounded woman learned in all ways, for I testify to you this day that security, true security comes from a knowledge of the divinity of Jesus Christ. This is the beginning of all learning and of all wisdom.

So, we turn now to the setting in which we can understand who the players are addressed by the first words spoken by Elohim in the endowment. As we look at the parties involved, ask yourself if the Holy Ghost confirms to your understanding the things that follow. If it does, then you have truth. If it does not, then you should discard it. But you must consult the witness of the Holy Ghost, and not your own prejudices or past understanding, to determine the truth.

Joseph Smith tried to identify the meaning of "God" during his final year in Nauvoo. He was excited about his expanding understanding of the nature and identity of God. He wanted to share the new insight, and first raised the subject in the April General Conference in a talk known as *The King Follett Discourse*. Then he returned again to the subject ten days before his death in June, 1844. His final June talk was cut short by rain, and he never finished his discussion. But we have enough from his comments to be able to know he was speaking from his translation of the Book of Abraham. To see what his comments drew from, first I'm going to set out the text from the Book of Abraham that provoked his excitement.

In order to expose how these scriptures speak about two different groups, I have identified them using highlighting in two different ways to make recognizing them easier. In bold below, the group known as "the noble and great" who are later referred to as "the Gods" are identified. In the italics below is the second group, who are being "proven" by the experience here in mortality. The mission assigned to each of these two groups is distinct. One is "proving" and the other is being "proven." The import of this is so profound that we should give a great deal of attention to it. It redefines what this estate is all about. It also caused Joseph Smith to make stunning remarks to the Saints in his last public address.

Both those who are identified as "noble and great" who are also called "Gods" are mortals here in this life, as well as those who are the "spirits organized before the world was" to be proven by this life. These two very different groups are both here in this world. For those who are being "proven" this life is a probation. For the others, they are "proving" their fellow men. The missions are quite different for these two groups. However, since there is a veil between here and there, the only way to know if you belong to one group or the other is if someone who is on the other side of the veil reveals it to you.

So first, we consider the scripture, using the highlighting to point out the two groups:

> 19 And the Lord said unto me: These two facts do exist, that there are two spirits, one being more intelligent than the other; there shall be another more intelligent than they; I am the Lord thy God, I am more intelligent than they all.[7]

> 20 The Lord thy God sent his angel to deliver thee from the hands of the priest of Elkenah.

> 21 I dwell in the midst of them all; I now, therefore, have come down unto thee to declare unto thee the works which my hands have made, wherein my wisdom excelleth them all, for I rule in the heavens above, and in the earth beneath, in all wisdom and prudence, over all the intelligences thine eyes have seen from the beginning; I came down in the beginning in the midst of all the intelligences thou hast seen.

> 22 Now the Lord had shown unto me, Abraham, the intelligences that were organized before the world was; and among all these there were **many of the noble and great ones;**

---

[7]   In his 16 June 1844 talk, ten days prior to his death, Joseph refers to this information from the Book of Abraham.

23 And God saw **these souls** that **they** were good, and he stood in the midst of **them**, and he said: **These** I will make my rulers; for he stood among those that were spirits, and he saw that **they** were good; and he said unto me: **Abraham, thou art one of them**; thou wast chosen before thou wast born.

24 And there stood one among **them** that was like unto God, and he said unto **those who were with him: We** will go down, for there is space there, and **we** will take of these materials, and we will make an earth whereon *these* may dwell;

25 And **we** will prove *them* herewith, to see if *they* will do all things whatsoever the Lord their God shall command *them*;

26 And they who keep their first estate shall be added upon; and they who keep not their first estate shall not have glory in the same kingdom with those who keep their first estate; and they who keep their second estate shall have glory added upon their heads for ever and ever.

27 And the Lord said: Whom shall I send? And one answered like unto the Son of Man: Here am I, send me. And another answered and said: Here am I, send me. And the Lord said: I will send the first.

28 And the second was angry, and kept not his first estate; and, at that day, many followed after him. [This is a third group, about whom I am not going to comment in this talk. However, I would note this is the "third" who followed the Dragon, is not a numeric calculation or percentage, but a way of distinguishing yet a third type of person who appears here on the earth.]

Abraham 3:19-28

1 AND then **the Lord said: Let us go down**. And **they** went down at the beginning, and they, **that is the Gods**, organized and formed the heavens and the earth.

2 And the earth, after it was formed, was empty and desolate, because **they** had not formed anything but the earth; and darkness reigned upon the face of the deep, and the Spirit of the Gods was brooding upon the face of the waters.

3 And **they (the Gods)** said: Let there be light; and there was light.

4 And **they (the Gods)** comprehended the light, for it was bright; and they divided the light, or caused it to be divided, from the darkness.

5 And **the Gods** called the light Day, and the darkness **they** called Night. And it came to pass that from the evening until morning **they** called night; and from the morning until the evening **they** called day; and this was the first, or the beginning, of that which **they** called day and night.

6 And **the Gods** also said: Let there be an expanse in the midst of the waters, and it shall divide the waters from the waters.

7 And **the Gods** ordered the expanse, so that it divided the waters which were under the expanse from the waters which were above the expanse; and it was so, even as **they** ordered.

8 And **the Gods** called the expanse, Heaven. And it came to pass that it was from evening until morning that **they** called night; and it came to pass that it was from morning until evening that **they** called day; and this was the second time that **they** called night and day.

Abraham 4:1-8

When the various groups are identified by highlighting, it becomes apparent that there are two kinds of mortals here. One type has already been called "Gods" in scripture. They are among those who have a calling to teach truth here. They are "noble and great" because they teach truth. They teach truth, and know truth, because they were of such a character before they came here that they had accepted, obeyed and received the results of following truth. In a word, they were exalted before they were born here. Hence the need for the word "Elohim" to be plural.

However radical an idea this may seem to you as you first hear it, Joseph Smith was trying to teach this to the Saints in Nauvoo. So we turn to Joseph's comments, first from the April General Conference talk. In this talk he introduces the concept of co-eternal existence for mankind as well as for God. He is introducing the notion that mankind has a higher or greater kind of existence than we may apprehend. Below are accounts first from Willard Richards, second Wilford Woodruff, and then finally from Thomas Bullock. I am leaving out the reports of George Laub and William Clayton.

Willard Richards' Account[8]

(The talk took from approximately 3:15 pm to 5:30 pm):

3 1/4 P. M.Joseph commenced speaking on the subject of the Dead relative to the death of elder King Follett who who was crushed in a well. by the falling of a tub of rock on him.

If men do not comprehend the character of God they do not comprehend themselves. what kind of being is God? Eternal life to know God. **if man does not know**

---

[8]   Joseph Smith Diary by Willard Richards; *The Words of Joseph Smith: The Contemporary Accounts of the Nauvoo Discourses of the Prophet Joseph, compiled and edited by Andrew F. Ehat and Lyndon W. Cook*, 340-343.

God, has not Eternal life.if I am so fortunate as to comprehend and explain the [incomplete thought] let evry one sit in silence and never lift your voice against the servants of God again.

Every man has a right to be a false prophet. as well as a true prophet. in the beginning. before the world was. **Is a man like one of yourselves. should you see him to day. you would see a man in fashion and in form**. Adam was formed in his likeness. refute the idea that God was God from all eternity Jesus said as the father had power in himself even so hath the son power to do what the father did. Lay down his body. & take it up again. **you have got to learn how to make yourselves God, Kings, Priests, &c. by going from a small to great capacity. Till they are able to dwell in everlasting burning & everlasting power**. how consoling when called to part with a dear friend. to know their very being will rise to dwell in everlasting burning. heirs of God. and **ascend a throne as those who have gone before**. I saw the father work out his kingdom with fear & trembling. god is glorified in salvation Exaltation of his ancestors &c. not all to be comprehended in this world. the head, or the head **one The head one of the Gods, brought forth the Gods**. Dr & Lawyers that have persecuted. **The head one called the Gods together in grand council to bring forth the world**. Example of error as yocabem Jacob the son of Zebedee & James James the son of Zebedee 4 Mat. 21. Greek Hebrew. German. & Latin. **In the begining the head of the gods called a council of the Gods and concocted a scheme to create the world**. Soon as we begin to understand the character of the Gods he begins to unfold the heavens to us. Doctors say. created the earth out of nothing. Borau. **creates. it means to organized. God had materials to organise the world**. Elements nothing can destroy. no beginning no end. The soul. Doctors of Divinity. God created in the beginning he never the character of man. don't believe it. who told you God was self existent? correct enough.in hebrew put into him his spirit. which was created before. **Mind of man coequal with God himself.** friends seperated for a small moment from **their spirits. coequal with God**. and hold converse when they are one with another **If man had a beginning he must have an end. might proclaim. God never had power to create the spirit of man. Inteligence exist upon a self existent principle no creation about it.** all mind & spirit God ever sent into the world are susceptible of enlargement.all things God has seen fit proper to reveal while dwelling in mortality, are revealed. precisely the same as though we were destitute of bodies. what will save our spirits will save our bodies our tabernacles for our spirits All spirits who have not obeyed the Gospel must be damned.who have not obeyed the decrees of son of man. We are looked upon by God as though we were in Eternity the greatest responsibility resting upon us is to look after our dead. they without us cannot be made perfect without us. Meet Paul 2 way. Hence the saying of Elijah. God made provisions before the world was for every creature in All sin shall be forgiven in this world or world to come except one Salvation for all men who have not committed a certain sin can save any man who has not committed the unpardonable sin. cannot commit the unpardonable sin after the dissolution of the body. Knowledge save a man. No way for a man to come to understanding but give his consent to the commandment Damned by mortification a lake as of fire of brimstone as exquisite the disappointment of the mind of man Why? Must commit the unpardonable sin in this world. will suffer in the eternal world until he will be exalted. work of the devil. the plans the devil laid to save the world. Devil said he could save them all Lot fell on Jesus. All sin &c forgiven except the sin against the Holy Ghost. Got to deny the plan of salvation. &c. with his eyes open. Like many of the apostates of christ of the Church of Jesus Christ of last Days. Let All be careful.lest you be deceived. best man brings forth best works. To the mourners your friend has gone to wait the perfection.of the reunion.the resurrection of your friend in felicity while worlds must wait myriads of years before they can receive the like blessings.leave the subject. bless those who have lost friends. only gone for a few moments. Shall mothers have their Children? Yes. they shall have it without price. redemption is paid possessing all the inteligence of a god. the child as it was before it died out of your arms thrones upon thrones. Dominion upon dominion just as you Baptism of water fire & Holy Ghost. are inseperably connected. found in the German Bible to prove what I have taught for 14 years about baptism.I baptize you with water. but when Jesus comes having the keys he shall baptize you with the baptism of fire & Holy Ghost. Leaving the principles of doctrine of baptism &c one god. one baptism. & one baptism I.E. all three. called upon all men. Priests and all to repent and obey the gospel.if they do not they will be damned.those who commit the unpardonable sin are doomed to Gnaolom. without end.God dwells in everlasting burnings. Love all men but hate your deeds. You don't know me you never will I don't blame you for not believing my history had I not experienced it could not believe it myself

5 2 closed.

Wilford Woodruff Diary[9]

3 o clock P M April Sunday 7th 1844

The following important edefying & interesting discourse was deliverd by President Joseph Smith to about twenty ten thousand souls upon the subject of the death of Elder King Follett.

---

9   Wilford Woodruff Diary, *The Words of Joseph Smith: The Contemporary Accounts of the Nauvoo Discourses of the Prophet Joseph,* compiled and edited by Andrew F. Ehat and Lyndon W. Cook, p.343, 344, 345, 346, 347-348.

I now call the attention of this congregation while I addres you upon the subject of the dead The case of our Beloved Brother King Follett, who was crushed to death in a well, as well as many others who have lost friends will be had in mind this afternoon, & shall speak upon the subject in general as far as I shall be inspired by the Holy Spirit to treat upon the subject it, I want the Prayers & faith of the saints that I may have the Holy Ghost, that the testimony may carry conviction to your minds of the truth of what I shall say, & pray that the Lord may strengthen my lungs, there is strength here & your prayers will be herd. Before I enter upon an investigation of this subject, I wish to pave the way, and bring up the subject from the beginning that you may understand. I do not intend to please you with oritory but with the simple truths of heaven to Edify you. Go to the morn of creation to understand of the decrees of the Eloheem at the Creation. It is necessary for us to have an understanding of God at the beginning, if we get a good start first we can go right, but if you start wrong you may go wrong. But few understand the character of God. they do not know they do not understand their relationship to God. the world know no more than the brute beast, & they know no more than to eat drink and sleep & this is all man knows about God or his exhistance, except what is given by the inspiration of the Almighty. go then to the beginning that you may understand. I ask this congregation **what kind of a being is God?** turn your thoughts in your hearts, & say have any of you seen or herd him or communed with him this is a question that may occupy your attention The scriptures inform us that this is eternal life to know the ownly wise God & Jesus Christ whom He has sent. If any inquire what kind of a being God is, I would say **If you don't know God you have not eternal life**, go back & find out what kind of a being God is. If I am the man that shows you what kind of a being God is, then let evry man & woman sit in silence and never lift up his hand against me again if I do not do it, I will not make any further pretentions to inspiration or to be a prophet, I would be like the rest of the world, fals teachers & you would want to take my life. But you might just as well take the lives of other fals teachers as mine if I was fals, But meddle not with any man for his religion, evry goverment ought to permit evry man to enjoy his religion, I will show the world is wrong by showing what God is. I am going to inquire after God so that you may know God, that persecution may cease concerning me, I go back to the beginning to show what kind of a being God was, I will tell you & hear it O Earth! **God who sits in yonder heavens is a man like yourselves That God if you were to see him to day that holds the worlds you would see him like a man in form, like yourselves.** Adam was made in his image and talked with him & walkd with him. In order to understand the dead for the consolation of those that mourn, I want you to understand God and how he comes to be God. **We suppose that God was God from eternity. I will refute that Idea, or I will do away or take away the veil so you may see.** It is the first principle to know that we may converse with him and that he once was a man like us, and the Father was once on an earth like us, And I wish I was in a suitable place to tell it The scriptures inform us mark it that Jesus Christ said As the Father hath power in himself so hath the son power in himself to do what the father did even to lay down my body & take it up again do you believe it, if not, don't believe the bible. I defy all Hell and earth to refute it. And **you have got to learn how to make yourselves God, king and priest, by going from a small capacity to a great capacity to the resurrection of the dead to dwelling in everlasting burnings,** I want you to know the first principle of this law, how consoling to the mourner when they part with a friend to know that though they lay down this dody [body]. it will rise & dwell with everlasting burnings to be an heir of God & joint heir of with Jesus Christ enjoying the same rise exhaltation & glory untill you arive at the station of a God. What did Jesus

Christ do, the same thing as I se the Father do, see the father do what, **work out a kingdom, when I do so to I will give to the father which will add to his glory, he will take a Higher exhaltation & I will take his place and am also exhalted.** Those are the first princples of the gospel. It will take a long time after the grave to understand the whole If I should say anything but what was in the bible the cry of treason would be herd I will then go to the Bible, Barasheet in the beginning, Analize the word in and through the head, an old Jew added the word Bath, it red **the head one of the Gods, broat forth the Gods,** I will transpose it in the english language. I want you to know & learn that the Holy Ghost knows somthing. The grand Council set [sat?] at the head and contemplated the creation of the world, some will say, the scriptures say so & so, but I will show you a text out of an old book containing the four languages, the german is here what does this text say, yoakabeam, the son of Zebedee, the bible says James the son of Zebedee, but this says Jacob son of Zebedee 21 ch 4th ver Matthew The Dr says (I mean Dr of Law not of physic) If you say any thing not according to the Bible we will cry treason, But if ye are not led by revelation how can ye escape the damnation of Hell, here we have the testimony of four I have the oldest Book in the world & the holy Ghost I thank God for the old Book but more for the Holy Ghost. **The Gods came together & concocked the plan of making the world & the inhabitants,** having an knowledge of God we know how to Approach him & ask & he will answer An other thing the learned Dr says the Lord made the world out of nothing, you tell them that God made the world out of somthing, & they think you are a fool. But I am learned & know more than the whole world, the Holy Ghost does any how, & I will associate myself with it. Beaureau, to organize the world out of chaotic matter, element they are principles that cannot be disolved they may be reoganized. Another subject which is calculated to exhalt man I wish to speak of The resurrection of the dead The soul the mind of man, whare did it come from? The learned says God made it in the beginning, but it is not so, I know better God has told me so. If you don't believe it, it wont make the truth without effect, **God was a self exhisting being, man exhists upon the same principle. God made a tabernacle & put a spirit in it and it became a Human soul, man exhisted in spirit & mind coequal with God himself,** you who mourn the loss of friends are ownly seperted for a moment, the spirit is seperated for a little time, they are now conversant with each other as we are on the earth. I am dwelling on the immutibility of the spirit of man, **is it logic to say the spirit of man had a begining & yet had no end, it does not have a begining or end, my ring is like the Exhistanc of man it has no begining or end, if cut into their would be a begining & end, so with man if it had a begining it will have an end, if I am right I might say God never had power to create the spirit of man, God himself could not create himself. Intelligence is Eternal & it is self exhisting,** All mind that is susseptible of improvement, the relationship we have with God places us in a situation to advance in knowledge. God has power to institute laws to instruct the weaker intelligences that thay may be exhalted with himself this is good d doctrin, it taste good, I can taste the principles of eternal life, so can you, they are given to me by the revelations of Jesus Christ and I know you believe it. All things that God sees fit to reveal to us in relation to us, reveals his commandments to our spirits, and in saving our spirits we save the body, the same as though we had no Body how comes the awful responsibility if in relation to our dead, if they do not be baptized they must be damned, (I wish I had 40 days to talk) what promises are made, what can be said if in the grave, God dwells in eternity, and he does not view things as we do, the greatest responsibility lade upon us in this life, is in relation to our dead Paul said we cannot be made perfect without us [them], for it is necessary that the seals are in our hands to seal our children & our dead for the fulness of the dispensation of times, A dispensation to meet the promises made by Jesus Christ befor the foundation of the world for the salvation of man. All sins and blasphemy, were to be forgiven except the sin against the Holy Ghost. God has made provision for evry spirit in the eternal world, and the spirits of our friends should be searched out & saved, Any man that has a friend in eternity can save him if he has not committed the unpardonable sin, He cannot be damned through all eternity, there is a possibility for his escape in a little time, If a man has knowledge he can be saved, if he has been guilty of great sins he is punished for it, when he consents to obey the gospel whether Alive or dead, he is saved, his own mind damns him I have no fear of hell fire that don't exhist No man can commit the un-pardonable sin, untill He receives the Holy Ghost, All will suffer untill they obey Christ himself, even the devil said I am a savior and can save all, he rose up in rebelion against God and was cast down,. Jesus Christ will save all except the sons of perdition. What must a man do 10 commit the unpardonable sin they must receive the Holy Ghost have the heavens opened unto them, & know God, & then sin against him, this is the case with many apostates in this Church, they never seease to try to hurt me, they have got the same spirit the devil had, you cannot save them, they make open war like the devil, stay all that hear, don't make any hasty mooves you may be saved, if a spirit of Bitter-ness is in you, don't be in haste, say you that man is a sin-ner, well if he repents he shall be forgiven. I could go back and trace evry subject of interest concerning the relation-ship of man to God if I had time, there is many mansions in my fathers Kingdom, What have we to console us in relation to our dead, we have the greatest hope in relation to our dead, of any people on earth we have seen them walk worthy on earth and those who have died in the faith are now in the selestial kingdom of God, they have gone to await the resurrection of the dead, to go to the celestial glory, while there is many who die who will have to wait many years, But I am authorized to say to you my friends in the name of the Lord, that you may wait for your friends to come forth to meet you in eternity in the morn of the celestial world, those saints who have been murdered in the persecution shall triumph in the celestial world, while their murderers shall dwell in torment untill they pay the utmost farthing.

I have Fathers, Brothers, children, that are gone to eternity soon to meet me, the time will soon be gone, the trump will soon be blown. A question will Mothers have their children in Eternity yes, yes, you will have the children But as it falls so it will rise, It will never grow, It will be in its precise form as it fell in its mothers arms. Eternity is full of thrones upon which dwell thousands of children reigning on thrones of glory not one cubit added to their stature I will leave this subject here and make a few remarks upon Baptism, I will read a tex[t] in Jerman [German] upon Baptism, John says I Baptise you with water But when Jesus Christ Comes He shall adminster the baptism of fire & the Holy Ghost, John said his baptism was good for nothing without the Baptism of Jesus Christ, Many talk of any baptism not being essential to salvation but this would lay the foundation of their damnation, There has also been remarks made concerning all men being redeemed from Hell, But I say that any man who commits the unpardonable sin must dwell in hell worlds without end.

Thomas Bullock's Account[10]

The President having arrived the Choir sung an hymn Elder Amasa Lyman prayed.

---

[10]   Thomas Bullock Report , *The Words of Joseph Smith: The Contemporary Accounts of the Nauvoo Discourses of the Prophet Joseph,* compiled and edited by Andrew F. Ehat and Lyndon W. Cook, p.348-349, 350, 351, 352.

The Prophet while I address you on the subject which was contempd in the fore pt. of the Con. as the Wind blows very hard it will be hardly possible for me to make you all hear it is of the greatest importance & the mo solemn of any that cod. occupy our attentn. & that is the subj of the dead on the dece of our bror. Follit who was crushed to death in a well& inasmuch as there are a great many in this congre who live in this city & who have lost friend I shall speak in genl. & offer you my ideas so far as I have ability & so far as I shall be inspd. by the H S. to dwell on his subjt. I want your prayer faith the inspn. of Alm God to say things that are true & shall carry the testimony to your hearts & pray that he may streng my lungs stay the winds& let the pray of the Saints to heaven appear for the prayers of the righteous avail much & I verily believe that your prayers shall be heard before I enter in this investign. fully of the subjt. that is lying before us I wish to make a few preliminaries in order that you may understand when I come to it I do not calculate to please your ears with oratory with much leang. but I calculate to edify you with simple truths from Heaven. **I wish to go back to the begin: of creation it** is necessary to know the mind decree & ordinatn. of the great Eloi beging at the creatn. & it is necy. for us to have un understandg. of God in the beging. if we start right it is very easy for us to go right all the time but if we start wrong it is hard to get right There are very few who understand rightly the char of GodThey do not comprehend any thing that is past or that which is to come & com: but little more than the brute beast if a man learns know nothing more than to eat, drink, sleep, & does not comprehend any of the desn. of God the Beast com the same thing eats drin sleeps[k]noes nothing more & how are we to do it by no or. way than the inspn of A. God.

I want to go back to the begin & so get you into a more lofty sphere than what the human being generally understands I want to ask this cong: every man wom:

& child to ansr. the questn. in their own heart what kind of a being is God I agn. rept. the questn. **what kind of a being is God** does any man or woman know have any of you seen, him heard him, communed with him, here is the questn. that will peradventure from this time henceforth occupy your attentn. The Apos: says this is Eternal life to know God & J.C. who he has sent that is eternal. life if any man enquire what kind of a being is God if he will search deligently his own heart that unless he knows God he has no eternal lifemy first object is to find out the character of the true God & if I shod. be the man to com: the God & I com: them to your heart let every man & woman henceforth shut their mouths & never say anything agst. the man of God & If I do not do it I have no right to revn. inspn. if all are [indecipherable word] to the God they will all be as bad off as I am. they will all say I ought to be d d. there is not a man or wom who wod not breath out an anathema on my head & some wod feel authd. to take away my lifeif any man is authd. to take away my life who say I am a false teacher so I shod. have the same right to all false teacher & where wod. be the end of the blood & there is no law in the heart of God that wod. allow any one to interfere with the rights of man every man has the right to be a false as well as a true prophetIf I shew verily that I have the truth of God & shew that ninety nine of 100 are false prop. it wod. deluge the whole world with blood. I want you all to know God to be familiar with him & if I can bring you to him all persecut. agst. me will cease & let you know that I am his servt. for I speak as one havg. authy. and not as a scrib[e] open your ears & eyes all ye Ends of the Earth & hear & I am going to prove. it to you with the Bible & I am going to tell you the desns. of God to the human race & why he interferes with the affairs of man **God himself who sits enthroned in yonder Heavens is a man like unto one of yourselves who holds this world in its orbit & upholds all things by his power if you were to see him today you wod. see him a man** for Adam was a man like in fashion & image like unto him Adam wakd talked & convd. with him as one man talks & com: with anor. in order to speak for the consoln. of those who mourn for the loss of their friend it is necy. to understand the char. & being of God for I am going to tell you what sort of a being of God. for he was God from the begin of all Eternity & if I do not refute ittruth is the touchstone they are the simple and first princ: of truth to know for a certainty the char. of God that we may conv[erse] with him same as a man & **God himself the father of us all dwelt on a Earth same as Js. himself did** & I will shew it from the BibleI wish I had the trump of an Arch An. I cod. tell the story in such a manner that pers: shod cease for everJ. Sd. as the Far. hath power in himself even so hath the Son power to do what the Far. did that ansr. is obvious in a manner to lay down his body & take it up Jdid as my Far. laid down his body & take it up agn. if you don't believe it you don't believe the Bile the Scrip says & I defy all hell all learng. wisdom & records of hell togr to refute it here then is Etl. life to know the only wise and true God **you have got to learn how to be a God yourself & be a K. & God Priest to God same as all have done by going from a small capy to anr. from grace to grace until the resn.** of & sit in everlasting power as they who have gone before & God in the L D. while certn. indivals are proclaimg. his name is not trifling with ushow consoling to the mourner when they are cald. to part with a wife, mother, father dr. relative to know that all Earthly taber shall be dissolved that they shall be heirs of God & jt. hrs of J. C. to inherit the same power exaltn. until you ascd. the throne of Etl. power same as those who are gone bef. what J. did I do the things I saw my Far. do before worlds came rolld. into existence I saw my Far. work out his K with fear & trembling & I must do the same when I shall give my K to the Far. so that he obtns K rollg. upon K. so that J treads in his tracks as he had gone before. It is plain beyond comprehensn. & you thus learn the first prin of the Gospel when you climb a ladder you must begin at the bottom run[g] until you learn the last prin of the gospel for it is a great thing to learn Saln. beyond the grave & it is not all to be com in this world. I sup I am not alld. to go into investign. but what is contd. in the Bible & I think there is so many wise men who wod. put me to death for treason I shall turn commentator today. I shall go to the first Hebrew word in the Bible the 1st sen: In the beginning Berosheat In by thro. & every thing else. Roshed the head when the Inspd. man wrote it he did not put the 1st pt. to it. a man a Jew witht. any authy. thot. it too bad to begin to talk about the head of any man. **"The Head one of the Gods brought forth the Gods"** is the true meang. of the wordif You do not believe it you do not believe the learned man of God no man can tell you more than I do thus **the H God brot. forth the Gods in the Head councill** want to bring it to English. Oh ye lawyers ye doctors I want to let you know that the H G. knows something as well as you **do the Head God called togr. the Gods & set in Grand Council** &c when I say a lawyer I mean a lawyer of the Scrip. I have done so hither to let the lawyers flutter & let everybody laugh at them. some learned Dr. mit. take a notn. to say thus & so& are not to be alto. & I am going to shew you an error I have an old book in the Latin Greek Hebrew & German & I have been readg. the Germ: I find it to be the most correct that I have found & it corresponds the nearest to the revns. that I have given the last 16 yrs 72 years it tells about Jachabod means Jacobin the English James& you may talk about James thro all Eternity in the 21 v. of 4th Mat: where it gives the test. that it is to Jacob & how can we escape the dn. of hell witht. God reveal to us. Latin says that Jackobus means JacobHebrew says means JacobGreek says Jacob German says Jacob thank God I have got this book & I thank him more for the gift of the H G. I have all the 4 Test. come here ye learned men & read if you can. I shod. not have brot. up this word unt only to shew that I am right when we beg to learn in this way **we beg to learn the only true God & when we be[g]in to know how to come to him he begins to unfold the heavens to us & tell us all abt. it** bef our prayers get to his ears at the bo now I ask all the learned men who hear me wher. the learned men who are preachg. Saln. say that God created the Heavens & the Earth out of nothing & the reason is that they are unlearned & I know more than all the world put togr. & If the H.G. in me com: more than all the world I will associate with itWhat does Boro mean it means to organize same as you wod. organize a Ship. **God himself had materials to org. the world out of chaos which is Element & in which dwells all the glorythat nothing can destroy they never can have an ending they coexist eternally** I have anor. to dwell on & it is impossible for me to say much but to touch upon themfor time will not permit me to say allso I must come to the resn. of the deadthe soul the in[ne]r Spiritall man says God created in the beging. the very idea lessens man in my ideaI don't bel. the doct: hear it all ye Ends of the World for God has told me so I am going to tell of things more **noble we say that God himself is a self-existing God**, who told you so, how did it get it into your head who told you that man did not exist in like manner how does it read in the Heb. that God made man & put into it Adams Spirit & so became **a living Spirit the mind of man the mind of man is as immortal as God himself** hence while I talk to these mourners they are only separated from their bodies for a short period their **Spirits coexisted with God** & now converse one another same as we dodoes not this give your satisfactn. I want to reason more on the Spirit of Man for I am dwelling on the body of man on the subjt. of the dead the SP of man **I take my ring from my finger and liken it unto the mind of man, the im[mor]t. Sp. bec. it has no beging**. Suppose you cut it into but as the D[evil] lives there wod. be an end all the fools & wise men from the beging. of creation **who say that man had begin they must have an end & then the doc of anni-**

hilitn. wod. be true but if I am right I mit. with bold-
ness proclaim from the housetop that God never had
power to create the Sp of Man at allit is ne God himself cod. not create himself intelligence is self existent it is a sp. from age to end & there is no creatn abt.
it the first principles of man are self exist with God-
that God himself finds himself in the midst of Sp &
bec he saw proper to institute laws for those who were
in less intelligence that they mit. have one glory upon
another in all that knowledge power & glory & so took
in hand to save the world of Sp: you say honey is Sweet
& so do I. I can also taste the Sp of Eternal life I know it is
good & when I tell you of these things that were given me
by Insp of the H S. you are bound to rece it as sweet & I
rej more & more. Mans rel. to God & I will open your eyes
in rel to your dead all things which God of his inf reason
has seen fit to reveal to us in our mortal state in regard to
our mortal bodies are revd. to us as if we had no bodies &
those revns. which will save our dead will save our bodies.
& God reveals them to us in the view of no eternal dissn.
of the body hence the awful responsibility that rests upon
us for our dead for all the Spirits must either obey the gospel or be dd solemn thot. dreadful thot. is there nothing to
be done for those who have gone before us without obeyg
the decrees of God Wod. to God that I had 40 days &
nights to tell you all to let you know I am not a faln prop
what kind of characters are those who can be saved altho
their bodies are decaying in the grave the greatest responsibility that God has laid upon us to seek after our dead the
apostle says they without us cant be Perfect now I am
speaking of them I say to you Paul, you cant be perfect
witht. us.those that are gone before & those who come
after must be made perfect& God has made it obligatory to
man God said he shall send Elijah &c I have a declarn to
make as to the provn. which God made from before the
foundn. of the world. what has J. sd. All sins & all blas.
every trans. that man may be guilty of there is a Saln. for

him or in the world to come every Sp in the Et. world can be ferreted out & saved unless he has comd. that Sin which cant be remd to him that God has wrot. out saln. for all men unless they have comd. a certn. sin. a friend who has got a friend in the world can save him unless he has comd. the unpard sin & so you can see how far you can be Savior there is no thing that a man can commit the unpardonable sin after the dissn of the body & there is a way possible for escape. not Part[icul]arly st[ate]d those that are witht. wisdom until they get exalted to wisdom so long as man will not give acct. of his sins a sinner has his own mind & is in his own comdemner for the G will the torment of the mind of man is as exquisite as a lake burng. with fire & brimstone I know the Scriptures I understand them no man can commit the unpardonable sin after the dissn. of the body but they must do it in this World hence the Saln. of J. C was wrought out for all men to triumph over the devil for he stood up for a SaviorJ. contd. that there wod. be certn. souls that wod. be condemned & the d[evi]l sd. he cod. save them allas the grand council gave in for J. C. so the d I fell & all who put up their heads for him. All sin shall be forgiven except the sin agt. the H. G. he has got to say that the Sun does not shine while he sees it he has got to deny J. C. when the heavens are open to him. & from that time they begin to be enemies like many of the apostates of the Church of J. C. of L.D.S. when a man begins to be an enemy he hunts him for he has the same Sp. that they had who crucd. the Lord of life the same Sp. that Sin agt. the H. G. I advise all to be careful what you do stay do not give way you may find that some one has laid a snare for you be cautious await when you find a Sp. wants bloodshed murder same is not of God but is of the devil out of the abundance of the heart man speaks the man that tells you words of life is the man that can save youI warn you agt all evil characters who sin agt. H. G. for there is no redempn. for them in this world nor in the world to come I can enter into the mysteriesI can enter largely into the eternal worlds-for J. sd. where my In my Fars. mansion there are many mansions &c There is one glory of the moon sun & star &c we have the reason to have the greatest hope & consoln. for our dead for we have aided them in the 1st princ for we have seen them walk in the midst & sink asleep in the arms of J. & hence is the glory of the Sun you mourners have occn. to rejoice for your husband has gone to wait until the redn. & your expn. & hope are far above what man can conceive for why God has revd. to us& I am authd. to say by the authy. of the H. G. that you have no occasn. to fear for he is gone to the home of the just don't mourn don't weepI know it by the test of the H. G. that is within me rejoice O Israel your friends shall triumph gloriously while their murderers shall welter for years.I say for the benefit of strangers I have a Far. Bror. Friends who are gone to a world of Sp they are absent for a momt. they are in the Sp. then shall we hail our Mor. Fars. Friends & all no fear of mobs&c but all one Eternity of felicity Mothers you shall have your Children for they shall have it for their debt is paid there is no damn. awaits them for they are in the Spirits as the Child dies so shall it rise from the ded & be living in the burng. of God. it shall be the child as it was bef it died out of your arms Children dwell & exercise power in the same form as they laid them down.

The Bap of Water witht. the B of Fire & the H G. attg. it are necy he must be born of W. & Sp in order to get into the K of God & in the German text bears me out same as the revns. which I have given for the 14 yearsI have the test to put in their teeth that my test has been true all the time You will find it in the declar of John the Bap (reads from the German) John says I bap you with Water but when J comes who has the power he shall adm the bap of F & the H. G. Gt. God now where is all the Sect. world. & if this is true they are all dd as clearly as any Anathama ever wasI know the text is trueI call upon all to say I (shouts of I) Alex Campbell how are you going to save them with water for John sd. his bapm. was nothing witht. the bap of J. C. One God, Far., Jesus, hope of, our calling, one baptism all three bap make one. I have the truth & I am at the defiance of the world to contradict. I have preached Latin Hebrew Greek German & I have fulfilled all I am not so big a fool as many have taken me for the Germans know that I read the German correctHear it all ye Ends of the Earth all ye Sinners Repent Repent turn to God for your reln. wont save you & ye will be dd but I do not say how along but those who Sin agt. the H. G. cannot be forgiven in this world or in the world to come but they shall die the 2nd. death but as they concoct scenes of bloodshed in this world so they shall rise to that resurn. which is as the lake of fire & brimstone some shall rise to the everlasting burning of God & some shall rise to the dn. of their own filthiness same as the lake of fire & brimstone I have intd. my remarks to all to all rich & poor bond & free great & small I have no enmity agst any man. I love you allI am their best friend & if persons miss their mark it is their own fault if I reprove a man & he hate me he is a fool for I love all men especially these my brethren & sistersI rejoice in hearing the test of my aged friend You never knew my heart. No man knows my histI can not do it. I shall never undertake if I had not experienced what I have I should not have known it myself I never did harm any man since I have been born in the world my voice is always for peaceI cannot lie down until my work is finishedI never think evil nor think any thing to the harm of my fellow man & when I am called at the trump & weighed in the balance you will know me then I add no more God bless you. Amen. The choir sung an hymn at 2 p 5.

These comments were made in April. By June, Joseph was ready to take the subject up again and elaborate on what was first introduced during the King Follett Discourse. His comments in June appear below. First, the quote found in the *Teachings of the Prophet*

Joseph Smith, which is accepted by the church as an authoritative source. There we find this quote: "I will preach on the plurality of Gods. I have selected this text for that express purpose. **I wish to declare I have always and in all congregations when I have preach on the subject of the Deity, it has been the plurality of Gods**. It has been preached by the Elders for fifteen years." (*TPJS*, 370.)[11]

The more complete account from which the comment was taken came from Thomas Bullock, a scribe for Joseph Smith at the time the talk was given. This report is set forth more fully below. In the more extended account below, Joseph tells us that his information about plurality of Gods came from translating the Book of Abraham, the source we quoted above. Here, then, are Joseph's final comments on this subject, given just ten days before his death:

Bullock's More Complete Report[12]

(16 June 1844 (1) (Sunday Morning). Grove East of Temple.)

Prayer by N Whitney choir sang "Mortals Awake" The Prophet read the 3rd Rev. text 6th. v. & made us K & P. unto God & his Far to him be glory & dom. for evermore. It is altogr. correct in the translatn. now you know that of late some have sprung up & apostat. & they declare that Pro bel[ieves]. in a plurality of Gods &c. & behold a very great secret they cry it has been my intentn. to take up this subjt. & show what my Faith is in the matterI have contemplated the saying of Je[sus] as it was in the days of Noah so shall it be at his 2nd. coming & if it rains I'll

---

[11]   Referring to *Lectures on Faith*, Lecture 5, paragraphs 1–2, as becomes apparent below.

[12]   Joseph Smith, *The Words of Joseph Smith: The Contemporary Accounts of the Nauvoo Discourses of the Prophet Joseph*, compiled and edited by Andrew F. Ehat and Lyndon W. Cook, 378-382.

preach the plurarlity of GodsI have selected this text I wish
to declare I have allways & in all congregats. when I have
preachcd it has been the plurality of Gods it has been
preached 15 yearsI have always decld. God to be a distinct
personageJ.C. a sep. & distinct pers from God the Far. the
H.G was a distinct personage & or Sp & these 3 constit. 3
distinct personages & 3 Gods if this is in accordance with
the New Test.lo & behold we have 3 Gods any how & they
are plural any how our text says the apost[les] have
disc[overe]d. that there were Gods above God was the Far.
of our Ld. J.C. my object was to preach the Scrip & preach
the doctrine there being a God above the Far. of our Ld.
J.C. I am bold to declare I have taut. all the strong doctrines
publicly & always stronger that what I preach in private
John was one of the men & the apos. declare they were
made K. & P. unto God the Fatr. of our Ld. J.C. it reads
just so hence the doctrine of a plurality of Gods is as
prominent in the Bible as any doctrine it is all over the face
of the Bible, it stands beyond the power of controversy a
wayfaring man tho a fool need not fail Paul says there are
gods many & Lords many I want to set it in a plain simple
manner but to us there is but one God pertaining to us, in
all thro all, but if J. Smith says there is Gods many & Lds.
many they cry away with him crucify him mankind verily
say that the Scrip [i]s with them Search the Script & & they
testify of things that apostates wod blaspheme Paul if Jo
Smith is a blasphemer you areI say there are Gods many &
Lds many but to us only one & we are to be in subject to
that one & no man can limit the bounds, or the eternal existence of eternal time hath he beheld the e[terna]l. world.
& is he authd. to say that there is only God he makes himself a fool & there is an end of his career in knowledge he
cannot obtn. all knowledge for he has sealed up the gate to
some say I do not interpret same as you they say it means
the heathen God. Paul says there are Gods many &c it
makes a plurality of Gods any how witht. a revn. I am not
going to give the God of Heaven to them any how you

know & I testify that Paul had no allusions to it I have it
from God & get over it if you can I have a witness of the
H.G & a test. that Paul had no allusion to the heathen G. in
the text Twice I will shew from the Heb. Bible & the 1st.
word shews a plurality of Gods & I want the apostate &
learned men to come here& prove to the contrary an unlearned boy must give you a little Hebrew Berosheit &c In
the begin. rosheit the head it shod. read the heads ofto organize the Gods Eloiheam Eloi. God in sing. heam, rean-
ders Gods I want a little learning as well as other fools

Popes quot: Drink deep all the confusion is for want of
drinking and draught the head God organized the heavens
& the Earth I defy all the learning in the world to refute me

In the begin the heads of the Gods organized the heaven &
the Earth now the learned Priest the people rage& the heathen imagine a vain thing if we pursue the Heb further it
reads:

The Head one of the Gods said let us make man in our
image I once asked a learned Jew once if the Heb. language
compels us to render all words ending in he am in the plural why not render the first plural he replied it would ruin
the Bible he acknowledged I was right. I came here to investigate these things precisely as I believe it hear & judge
for yourself & if you go away satisfied well & good in the
very beginning there is a plurality of Gods beyond the
power of refutation it is a great subject I am dwelling on
the word Eloiheam ought to be in the plural all the way
thro Gods the heads of the Gods appointed one God for
us & when you take a view of the subject it sets one free to
see all the beauty holiness & perfection of the God all I
want is to get the simple truth naked & the whole truth
Men say there is one God the Far. Son & the H.G. are only
1 God it is a strange God any how 3 in 1. & 1 in 3. it is a
curious thing any how Far. I pray not for the world but I
pray for those that thou givest me &c &c all are to be

crammed into 1 God it wod. make the biggest God in all
the world he is a wonderful big God he would be a Giant I
want to read the text to you myself I am agreed with the
Far. & the Far. is a greed with me & we are agreed as one
the Greek shews that is shod. be agreed Far. I pray for
them that thou hast given me out of the world &c &c that
they may be agreed & all come to dwell in unity & in all the
Glory & Everlasting burngs of God & then we shall see as
we are seen & be as God& he as the God of his Far.I want
to reason **I learned it by translating the papyrus now in
my house I learned a test. concerning Abraham & he
reasoned concerng. the God of Heaven**[13] in order to do
that sd. he suppose we have two facts that supposes that
anotr. fact may exist two men on the earth one wiser than
the other wod. shew that antr. who is wiser than the wisest
may exist intelligences exist one above anotr. that there is
no end to it if Abra. reasoned thus if J.C was the Son of
God & John discd. that god the Far. of J.C had a far. you
may suppose that he had a Far. also where was ther ever a
Son witht. a Far. where ever did tree or any thing spring
into existence witht. a progenitor& every thing comes in
this way Paul says that which is Earthly is in likeness of
that which is Heavenly hence if J. had a Far. can we not
believe that he had a Far. also I despise the idea of being
scared to deathI want you all to pay particr. attent. J. sd. as
the Far. wrought precisely in the same way as his Far. had
done bef as the Far. had done bef. he laid down his life &
took it up same as his Far. had done bef he did as he was
sent to lay down his life & take it up again & was then
committed unto him the keys &c I know it is good reason-
ingI have reason to think that the Church is being purged I
saw Satan fall from heaven& the way they ran was a caution. all these are wonders & marvellous in our eyes in
these last days so long as men are under the law of God
they have no fears, they do not scarce themselvesI want to

---

[13] See Abraham 3:19.

stick to my text to shew that when men open their lips they do not injure me but injure themselves To the law & to the testimony they are poured all over the Scrip When things that are great are passed over witht. even a thot I want to see all in all its bearings & hug it to my bosom I bel. all that God ever revd. & I never hear of a man being d[amne]d for belg. too much but they are dd for unbel. they found fault with J.C. bec. he sd. he was the Son of God & made himself equal with God they say like the apost. of old I must be put down what Je. say it is written in your law I said Ye are Gods it was thro' him that they drink of the rock of course he wod. take the honor to himself J. if they were called Gods unto whom the word of God why shld. it be thot incredible that I shod. say I am the Son of God. Oh Apostates did ye never think of this bef. these are the quotations that the apostates take to the Scrip they swear that they bel the Bible & the Book of Mormon &c & then you will get filth & slander & bogus makers plenty& one of the Church members prophesied that Jo Smith shld. never preach any more& yet I am now prachg. go & read the vision there is glory & glorySun, moon & Stars& so do they differ in glory & every man who reigns is a God& the text of the Do & Covt damns themselvesPaul what do you say they impeached Paul & all Went & left him Paul had 7 churches & they drove him off from among them& yet they cannot do it by me I rej. in that my test. is good Paul says there is one Glory of the Sun the moon & the Stars& as the Star differs &c They are exalted far above princ. thrones dom. & angels & are expressly decld. to be heirs of God & jt. heirs with J.C. all havg. et[erna]l. power the Scrip are a very strange doct. I have an[othe]r. Scrip now says God when visited Moses in the Bush moses was a stutt[er]ing sort of a boy like me God said thou shalt be a God unto the children of Israel God said thou shalt be a God unto Aaron & he shall be thy spokes. I bel. in these Gods that God reveals as Gods to be Sons of God & all can cry Abba Father Sons of God who exalt themselves to

be Gods even from bef. the foundatn. of the world & are
all the only Gods I have a reverence for[14] John sd. he was a
K[ing]. J.C. who hath by his own blood made us K & P to
God. Oh thou God who are K. of K's & Ld. of Lds. we
cannot bel. thee old Catholic Church is worth more than all
here is a princ. of logic that men have no more senseI will
illustrate an old apple tree here jumps off a branch & says I
am the true tree. & you are corrupt if the whole tree is corrupt how can any true thing come out of it the char[acte]r
of the old ones have always been sland[ere]d. by all
apos[tates] since the world began I testify again as God
never will acknowledge any apost: any man who will betray
the Catholics will betray you & if he will betray one anothr.
he will betray you all men are liars who say that they are of
the true God always sent a new dispensatn. into the world-
when men come out & build upon o[the]r men's foundatn.
did I build on anotr. mans foundtn. but my own I have got
all the truth & an indepent. rev[elatio]n. in the bargain &
God will bear me off triumphantI will drop this subjt. I
wish I cod. speak for 3 or 4 hours it is not expedt. on acct.
of the rain I will still go on & shew you proof on proof. all
the Bible is as equal one part as anothr.

In the *Teachings of the Prophet Joseph Smith*, selected and
arranged by Joseph Fielding Smith, p. 74, we have this statement
drawn from the above material: "These Scriptures are a mixture of
very strange doctrines to the Christian world, who are blindly led by
the blind. I will refer to another Scripture. 'Now,' says God, when
He visited Moses in the bush, (Moses was a stammering sort of a
boy like me) God said, 'Thou shalt be a God unto the children of
Israel.' God said, 'Thou shalt be a God unto Aaron, and he shall be
thy spokesman.' I believe those Gods that God reveals as Gods to
be sons of God, and all can cry, 'Abba, Father!' Sons of God who

---

14   See Abraham 4:1–8.

exalt themselves to be Gods, even from before the foundation of the world, and are the only Gods I have a reverence for," an obvious reference to the doctrine he was then learning from the 3rd and 4th chapters of the Book of Abraham.

Well, Joseph did not have those 3 or 4 hours, and never returned to teach on the subject. We do have, however, other statements in scripture which also bear on the subject of mankind's potential godlike existence. For example, from Jesus Christ we have the following: (John 10:34) "Jesus answered them, Is it not written in your law, I said, Ye are gods?"

Then again we have Christ responding to a question in Luke 17:20-21: "And when he was demanded of the Pharisees, when the kingdom of God should come, he answered them and said, The kingdom of God cometh not with observation: Neither shall they say, Lo here! or, lo there! for, behold, the kingdom of God is within you." If it is within some (or maybe even all) of us, then we possess it already. We cannot possess it without having brought it with us from before.

The idea that we bring something eternal or possessing power with us from before this life is affirmed in Alma's teaching regarding high priesthood. He wrote the following:

> 2 And those priests were ordained after the order of his Son, in a manner that thereby the people might know in what manner to look forward to his Son for redemption.
>
> 3 And this is the manner after which they were ordained being called and **prepared from the foundation of the world according to the foreknowledge of God,** on account of their exceeding faith and good works; in the first place being left to choose good or evil; therefore they having chosen good, and exercising **exceedingly great faith,**

are called with a holy calling, yea, with that holy calling
which was prepared with, and according to, a preparatory
redemption for such.

4 And thus they have **been called to this holy calling on
account of their faith**, while others would reject the Spirit
of God on account of the hardness of their hearts and
blindness of their minds, while, if it had not been for this
they might have had as great privilege as their brethren.

5 Or in fine, in the first place they were on the same standing with their brethren; thus **this holy calling being prepared from the foundation of the world** for such as
would not harden their hearts, being in and through the
atonement of the Only Begotten Son, who was prepared

6 And thus being called by this holy calling, and ordained
unto the high priesthood of the holy order of God, to
teach his commandments unto the children of men, that
they also might enter into his rest

7 This high priesthood being after the order of his Son,
which order was **from the foundation of the world; or in
other words**, being without beginning of days or end of
years, being prepared from eternity to all eternity, according
to his foreknowledge of all things.

Alma 13:2-7

From these teachings we know that high priesthood relates back
to preparation and calling before the foundation of the world.
Those who inherit it here brought that right with them when they
came. This gives new meaning to two things: First, it shows why the
authority of the priesthood is something which can be conferred

upon anyone, but the power of priesthood is something which only a few will possess.[15]

In President Boyd K. Packer's General Conference address (April 2010) he spoke about the success the church has had in distributing the administrative authority of the priesthood throughout the world. But he lamented the failure to have the power of the priesthood spread co-equal with the authority. This may not be so much a failure of the church to discharge responsibility devolving upon it as it may be a failure of those who receive it here to have ever qualified in the first place to bear such priestly power. This, however, is off the main subject now being discussed. So we return to the main topic.

Joseph's comment about those who "exalted themselves to be gods before the world began" came after the full definition of exaltation was known. Indeed, the then most recent recorded revelation was what now appears as Section 132. It had been written down in its final form on July 12, 1843 and dealt with the definition of exaltation. Among other things that revelation contained the following language:

---

[15]   D&C 121:34-41: Behold, there are many called, but few are chosen. And why are they not chosen? Because their hearts are set so much upon the things of this world, and aspire to the honors of men, that they do not learn this one lesson That the rights of the priesthood are inseparably connected with the powers of heaven, and that the powers of heaven cannot be controlled nor handled only upon the principles of righteousness. That they may be conferred upon us, it is true; but when we undertake to cover our sins, or to gratify our pride, our vain ambition, or to exercise control or dominion or compulsion upon the souls of the children of men, in any degree of unrighteousness, behold, the heavens withdraw themselves; the Spirit of the Lord is grieved; and when it is withdrawn, Amen to the priesthood or the authority of that man. Behold, ere he is aware, he is left unto himself, to kick against the pricks, to persecute the saints, and to fight against God. We have learned by sad experience that it is the nature and disposition of almost all men, as soon as they get a little authority, as they suppose, they will immediately begin to exercise unrighteous dominion. Hence many are called, but few are chosen. No power or influence can or ought to be maintained by virtue of the priesthood, only by persuasion, by long-suffering, by gentleness and meekness, and by love unfeigned;"

16 Therefore, when they are out of the world they neither marry nor are given in marriage; but are appointed angels in heaven, which angels are ministering servants, to minister for those who are worthy of a far more, and an exceeding, and an eternal weight of glory.

17 For these angels did not abide my law; therefore, they cannot be enlarged, but remain **separately and singly, without exaltation,** in their saved condition, to all eternity; and from henceforth are **not gods, but are angels of God** forever and ever.

18 And again, verily I say unto you, if a man marry a wife, and make a covenant with her for time and for all eternity, if that covenant is not by me or by my word, which is my law, and is not sealed by the Holy Spirit of promise, through him whom I have anointed and appointed unto this power, then it is not valid neither of force when they are out of the world, because they are not joined by me, saith the Lord, neither by my word; when they are out of the world it cannot be received there, because the angels and the gods are appointed there, by whom they cannot pass; they cannot, therefore, inherit my glory; for my house is a house of order, saith the Lord God.

19 And again, verily I say unto you, if a man marry a wife by my word, which is my law, and by the new and everlasting covenant, and it is sealed unto them by the Holy Spirit of promise, by him who is anointed, unto whom I have appointed this power and the keys of this priesthood; and it shall be said unto themYe shall come forth in the first resurrection; and if it be after the first resurrection, in the next resurrection; and shall inherit thrones, kingdoms, principalities, and powers, dominions, all heights and depths then shall it be written in the Lamb's Book of Life, that he shall commit no murder whereby to shed innocent blood, and if ye abide in my covenant, and commit no murder whereby to shed innocent blood, it shall be done unto them in all

things whatsoever my servant hath put upon them, in time, and through all eternity; and shall be of full force when they are out of the world; and **they shall pass by the angels, and the gods, which are set there, to their exaltation and glory in all things, as hath been sealed upon their heads, which glory shall be a fulness and a continuation of the seeds forever and ever.**

20 Then shall they be gods, because they have no end; therefore shall they be from everlasting to everlasting, because they continue; then shall they be above all, because all things are subject unto them. Then shall they be gods, because they have all power, and the angels are subject unto them.

21 Verily, verily, I say unto you, except ye abide my law ye cannot attain to this glory.

22 For strait is the gate, and narrow the way that leadeth unto the exaltation and continuation of the lives, and few there be that find it, because ye receive me not in the world neither do ye know me.

23 But if ye receive me in the world, then shall ye know me, and shall receive your exaltation; that where I am ye shall be also.

24 This is **eternal lives** to know the only wise and true God, and Jesus Christ, whom he hath sent. I am he. Receive ye, therefore, my law.

25 Broad is the gate, and wide the way that leadeth to **the deaths**; and many there are that go in thereat, because they receive me not, neither do they abide in my law.

D&C 132:16-25

For those who qualified before this life to be "exalted" to meet the definition of the word, they must have been sealed into a family unit, husband and wife, possessing the capacity for the continuation of lives. This would mean, therefore, that the Elohim (being plural) included those who were parents. Parents whose decision to come here and prove their own children, required them to in turn come and minister here as servants for those children they hoped to redeem.

We have a very limited view of the workings of God among men. We have taken a Judeo-Christian view when we were meant to understand things which go far beyond anything these religious traditions have been able to retain. The Restoration of All Things was supposed to revolutionize our understanding. Just as the vision of the three degrees of glory (D&C Section 76) changes fundamentally the picture of the afterlife for us, so also Joseph's restoration of the record of Abraham changes our view of the pre-earth councils.

We should spend less time trying to harmonize our beliefs with mainstream Christianity and more time allowing what we have been given to inform us of things which we have never known.

Returning then to the first three words spoken by the players in the endowment: Elohim, who speaks, is not a solitary figure. At a minimum it is a couple, male and female. It may include, however, hundreds of others who qualified as both "noble and great" and "the Gods" before this earth was formed. The Elohim speak and say, first: "Jehovah." The first word spoken is the name of the Lord and Redeemer. Of a truth He is then the Word. He is the beginning of the words of God the Father or the Elohim. He is first. His role will be primary. Not just in creation, but also in redemption of that creation.

The Word, Jehovah, is followed by the name "Michael." Michael is 'simply symbolic so far as the man and woman are concerned.' Michael may be the name of a real pre-earth person, but here it is also a symbol for *all* those who are similarly situated. These would include both pre-earth men and women. All those who were 'noble and great' and destined to come and inhabit this world. These are all those who are called in Abraham chapter 4 "the Gods."

The third word spoken, after naming those to whom direction is being given, is a command to "see." It could be restated: "behold." Or "look." Or "open your mind to understand." Or, "lose your blindness and accept what is before you." No matter how you render it, the command remains one of the most important still for us to obey. We must be willing to "see." What we will see from the foregoing is this:

First, there are those who were identified as "the Gods" before the world was organized.

Second, there were those for whom this world was designed to be a time of "proving" and testing who were not identified as "the Gods" before the world was organized.

Third, Joseph regarded those who were identified as "the Gods" to be "sons of God who exalted themselves to be gods before the world was made."

Fourth, you cannot know the group to which you belong because there is a veil between all of us and the pre-earth existence. The risks of mortality, however, are the same for all who are here. The way back is the same no matter which group you belong to, and either can fall from their exaltation or can acquire their exaltation, depending entirely upon the kind of life they live here.

Fifth, only the Lord knows and can tell you of your pre-earth status. If you learn of that it will be only through revelation.

Sixth, nothing about this changes the risks of mortality or the obligations we owe to God while here. It should not change in any way the life you live. It may let you understand things differently, may give you more hope for things, or a deeper appreciation for some ideas, but it should not change how you understand your obligation to live your life and the risks of mortality.

I am hoping, however, that it gives you a new way to view the endowment and how much more we can see within it with a little effort to open our eyes, and follow the admonition from Elohim to "see."

ESSAY 2:
THE MISSION OF ELIJAH RECONSIDERED

THE MISSION OF ELIJAH RECONSIDERED

This paper continues the topic of Elijah's importance in the last days that was introduced in *Passing the Heavenly Gift*. I will assume the reader is familiar with the content of that book in this discussion, and will not repeat the background found there. Having illustrated my view of the inadequate and inaccurate understanding found in the traditional Latter-day Saint teaching, this paper will continue to set out my view of the topic, with an explanation of Elijah's future necessary role which must precede the Second Coming of Christ.

A great impediment to learning is fear. We need to discuss "fear" before introducing some additional thoughts about Elijah's mission. Elijah has a role in the last days. It was foretold by Malachi,[16] reiterated by Christ to the Nephites,[17] and promised by Moroni when he visited with Joseph Smith on September 21, 1823.[18]

---

[16] Mal. 4:5-6.

[17] 3 Ne. 25:5-6.

[18] See JS-H 1:12, D&C Section 2.

Although the tradition among Latter-day Saints is that this is a past event, having occurred in 1836;[19] in 1844 Joseph Smith spoke of it as yet future.[20] I hope you can consider these ideas without fear.

When you read a phrase in the scriptures that is repeated in almost identical language by John (1 John 4:18), Paul (2 Tim. 1:7) and Moroni (Moroni 8:16), it should leap out to your mind. These divergent personalities converge on the same thought, and to me it suggests something important and profound. I am going to use John's, found at 1 John 4:18: "there is no fear in love, but perfect love casteth out fear, because fear hath torment. He that feareth is not made perfect in love."

According to Joseph Smith, the Gospel of Jesus Christ comprehends [includes] all truth. (See 9 July 1843 Sermon at Nauvoo in *Words of Joseph Smith.*) It is fear that limits our capacity to gain from what God offers us in the Gospel. It is a measure of our ingratitude when we decline the invitation extended by Joseph[21] to search deeper and deeper into the mysteries of God, and instead elect to fearfully withdraw, concluding we are just not interested in what we might have had.[22]

It is a trick of the devil to get people to close their minds and close their hearts, because they fear what they may be learning will do damage to them.[23] When Adam and Eve partook of the fruit, and then Satan called their attention to the fact that they were na-

---

[19]   See D&C Section 110.

[20]   I assume the reader is familiar with the information contained in *Passing the Heavenly Gift*, in which Section 110 and Section 132 are carefully examined.

[21]   "I advise all to go on to perfection, and search deeper and deeper into the mysteries of Godliness." *TPJS*, 364.

[22]   See D&C 88:33.

[23]   See 2 Ne. 28:29-30.

ked,[24] that is the beginning of the mischief visited on humanity by the adversary who seeks to bind, control and limit the freedom of all mankind in order to imprison them.[25] He pointed out to them that they ought to be ashamed. Therefore, when they heard the voice of God speaking, they withdrew because of what the shame triggered within them—fear. They were ashamed to come into the presence of that being who they knew to be just and holy, because now they were naked and afraid.[26] Their "nakedness" before God came as a consequence of understanding the difference between what they were, compared to the perfection of God.[27] That knowledge came as a result of partaking out of season and sequence, of the fruit. They were not going to receive a command to partake of the fruit until after the day of rest had been observed. They were not only naked before God, but they were also violating the Sabbath. They were beginning the labor of mortal existence out of time, sequence and season. That is the way a great number of errors are made in mortality.

You see, we are commanded *not* to partake of some things out of season. Then we are commanded to partake within season.[28] When we get the timing wrong, we wind up with difficulties and problems we should not have encountered. When we make that

---

24   Gen. 3:7.

25   2 Ne. 2:18.

26   This is the reaction of any who come into God's presence in their fallen state. See Mormon 9:4-5.

27   *Id.*

28   "That which is wrong under one circumstance, may be, and often is, right under another. God said, 'Thou shalt not kill'; at another time He said, 'Thou shalt utterly destroy.' This is the principle on which the government of heaven is conducted—by revelation adapted to the circumstances in which the children of the kingdom are placed. Whatever God requires is right, no matter what it is, although we may not see the reason thereof till long after the events transpire." (*TPJS*, 256.)

mistake, we are forced to repent. Repentance is a critical thing. It is the message of the Book of Mormon. It is the greatest message contained in the book of Isaiah and it is the message of all true prophets.[29] There are two things that generally stir you up to repentance. The first thing is to awaken to your awful situation.[30] The second is to arise,[31] and connect with the source that will cure what is wrong with you. We are not self-curing. We are filled with that same shame that came in the beginning as a consequence of doing what we were not suppose to be doing. The greatest way the adversary keeps us in a state of slumber is to prevent us from looking about and awakening to the awful situation we find ourselves. Hugh Nibley commented on more than one occasion that there is nothing quite as annoying as being awakened out of a deep sleep.[32] No one really likes that. When it comes right down to it, unconsciousness is a very pleasurable thing; particularly when what you awaken to what we face here.

Alma the Younger is a fairly expert source on the subject of repentance. Alma the Younger, after he had been seasoned by his dramatic conversion,[33] his experience preaching the gospel,[34] and his experience as a father, gave some advice to his own children. He gave them a talk that included an explanation about the demands of justice on the one hand,[35] and mercy on the other,[36] and how they

---

[29]   See, e.g., 1 Ne. 1:4;Ether 11:20; Helaman 15:7 and D&C 11:9.

[30]   See, e.g., 2 Ne. 1:13; 4:28; 8:17, 24; Jacob 3:11.

[31]   See, e.g., 2 Ne. 1:14, 21; 8:25; Mosiah 2:32; Moroni 10:31.

[32]   See, e.g., *Last Call: An Apocalyptic Warning from the Book of Mormon*, p. 23.

[33]   See Mosiah Chapter 27, Alma Chapter 36.

[34]   See Alma Chapters 4-14.

[35]   Alma 42:13-14, 22.

[36]   *Id.* vs. 15, 23.

are balanced with one another so that mercy can overcome the demands of justice. It is not by robbing it.[37] It is by satisfying it.[38] It was a brilliant doctrinal discourse. It is followed by a series of statements at the end of his advice which we consider here. This is in chapter 42 of Alma. At the beginning of verse 27 he said, "Therefore, O my son, whosoever come may come and partake of the waters of life freely; and whosoever will not come the same is not compelled to come..." It is free, and not only is it free, it is non-compulsive.[39] It is purely voluntary. Anyone is free to accept it. Anyone is free to reject it. But in the last day, it shall be restored unto him according to his deeds. That is, offered freely, available to all, non-compulsory, but you are *accountable*. Therefore, when you decline what is offered to you, then you receive at the last day the recompense you merit because of your ingratitude. Those who refuse will receive whatever it is that comes as a consequence of their refusal. Those who receive, will receive what God offered. He continues:

> 28 If he has desired to do evil, and has not repented in his days, behold, evil shall be done unto him, according to the restoration of God.

> 29 And now, my son, I desire that ye should let these things trouble you no more, and only let your sins trouble you, with that trouble which shall bring you down unto repentance.

> Alma 42:28-29

---

37   *Id.* v. 25.

38   *Id.* v. 30.

39   See D&C 121:46.

Don't trouble yourself, unless it motivates you to change. Repentance means change. Repentance actually means you turn from the direction you are facing. Whatever direction you are facing turn from that and face God. When you turn to God and face Him, and let Him be the object of your focus and your attention, then you have repented. Facing your job, or your favorite sports team, or your religious hobby, or even your church leaders is not the same thing as facing God. He continues:

> 30 O my son, I desire that ye should deny the justice of God no more. Do not endeavor to excuse yourself in the least point because of your sins, by denying the justice of God; but do you let the justice of God, and his mercy, and his long-suffering have full sway in your heart; and let it bring you down to the dust in humility.
>
> Alma 42:30

Well that is a graphic expression: being "brought down to the dust." Dust is something that is below, beneath, on the ground. You have to grovel in order to get there. But that is the point. "Awaking and arising" always begins from the position of being in the dust. We are all in the dust anyway. Somehow we manage to ignore it. It is only by virtue of waking up and discovering that you happen to be in a rather dusty spot that you finally decide to get up and brush yourself off. That is the condition we find ourselves, as soon as we awaken to our awful situation.[40]

Therefore, when listening to the voices calling for your attention to whatever it is they want you to pay attention to in this world, Alma suggests it might be helpful to your eternal salvation is to listen to those who cry repentance. Those are the voices that happen to be saying something that deserves your attention. Repent!

---

[40] Ether 8:24.

Change the course you are on! Turn and face God! Allow the only one who can offer salvation to offer you salvation.

In *Ten Parables* there is a story of "Hope and Tarwater"—which by the way is a parable that has multiple meanings, but the intended meaning is that both Hope and Tarwater are the pre-existence. You run with that when you read it. Tonight, because parables allow you to shift meaning, what I would like the story to be about is the attitude you bring with you to any of life's circumstances. You likely bring your life's attitude from the pre-existence, but we'll confine tonight to the attitude you bring with you to anything you encounter in mortality. You see, what Lance found in the forest was exactly what Lance thought he would find in the forest. What James found in the forest was exactly what James thought he would find in the forest. Neither one of them could escape the view they brought with them into the condition they found themselves. It is a painful experience to realize that the way you have always understood the world is, in fact, skewed, amiss, ugly, wrong, deceived, and even malevolent. No one wants to encounter that, which makes change so terribly difficult for us.

When I was 19, the missionaries succeeded at last in overcoming my opposition to the message they taught. I used up, with liberal abandon, a great quantity of missionaries who came to teach me. I was a "golden contact" only because the mission field was comprised of a spiritually scurvy lot of hard-headed New Englanders, with no inclination to listen to what the Mormons had to say. I made the error of complimenting a fellow and being polite to their approach. It was mistaken as interest, and so they were fetching me with pamphlets, felt boards, slide strips and the paraphernalia used in those days. Though polite, I was not really interested. I literally showed up to a missionary discussion with a six pack of beer once.

I intended to share with the missionaries and LDS family whose home we were using. I also asked if I could light a cigar in the living room. I look back on that now and I cringe. I had no idea, because they hadn't gotten to the Word of Wisdom discussion as yet, so in my ignorance I was outside the correct behavioral lines. Well intentioned, but ignorant. There's a lot of that going on still, I suppose. Not because of bad intentions, but only because of my enduring ignorance. It is why, when we repent and face God, we tend to learn a great deal more than we know at the time.[41] God imparts intelligence, light and truth.[42] You cannot learn what He imparts if you refuse to face Him. When you strain His light through another man, even a very good man, you lose a vital connection we are all intended to possess.[43]

As the missionaries were teaching me, eventually something happened that got my attention. I began to entertain the idea that what these missionaries were saying may be the correct criteria to measure their message. The message they offered required an entire shift in my world view. I had been raised from my youth in Idaho to understand Joseph Smith was a charlatan and a fraud, and Mormons were deceived and misled into worshipping a false God, and so on. All the ridiculous and incorrect characterizations you hear in the religious (now even the political) debates of our country, I accepted.

Well, I had to make the leap from the world view of 'Lance in the forest' to the world view of 'James in the forest' in order to say "there might be something to this." That is the problem with the restored Gospel—there really might be something to it. And if there is something to this, then how important is it? And if it is that

---

[41]   D&C 50:24.

[42]   D&C 93:28, 36-37.

[43]   D&C 84:98.

important, then how thoroughly ought we all to examine it? How relentlessly ought we to search into it? And, how carefully ought we to consider it? If there is some additional light that can be shed about any topic relating to the restored Gospel, how freely, how openly ought we to discuss it? These are rhetorical questions, but they deserve our careful attention because we slam the door on some of these important matters long before we have even been informed on important topics. We are not much different than the unconverted. We plug our ears, close our eyes and declare "I have a testimony," thinking that is enough. Just because Joseph had a testimony at 15 years of age, he did not cut off additional enlightenment and correction. He continued to learn through his 38th year. Some of the greatest things he learned came late in the Nauvoo period, in the final months of his life. I've written an essay on the *First Three Words [Spoken by the Players in the Endowment]* which considers some of Joseph's last talks in Nauvoo. He was preoccupied by what he was learning about the creation through the Book of Abraham. He followed his own advice: "The things of God are of deep import and time and experience and careful and ponderous and solemn thoughts can only find them out. Thy mind O man if thou wilt lead a soul into salvation must search into and contemplate the darkest abyss and the broad expanse of eternity, thou must commune with God." (*DHC* 3:295.) He plumbed the depths of the Gospel and continued to search to the day he died.

I have no fear whatsoever about examining Joseph Smith from top to bottom, through and through, every minute of his life. I don't have any concerns about that. None of us should. He is the latest and best documented case of a prophet who had the heavens opened and the ministering of angels. Anyone who even pretends to be wise will seek to get informed by the things that came from his hands.[44]

I think anyone *un*willing to entertain a thorough examination of the life and ministry of Joseph Smith is demonstrating fear, which is the opposite of love. We don't have details about the life of Moses. We don't have details about the life of Peter. We have an extraordinary limited vantage point from which to examine either one of them. We don't have much in the way of detail about the life of Nephi. In fact, everything we have about Nephi is autobiographical and composed years after the events themselves.[45] Therefore, to some extent, Nephi is going to present a narrative that doesn't give a full, fair and impartial accounting of why his brothers continually found themselves not persuaded by the message he delivered. I understand there are always those who are hard-hearted. I understand there are natural resentments whenever a younger brother supplants the older brother. This would be particularly true when the supplanting takes place very early on in a difficult journey, as happened with Nephi, Laman and Lemuel. Nephi returned with the emblems of kingship (the sword of Laban, the brass plates, and the servant of Laban's—Zoram). Then during the trek in the wilderness he actually assumes the role, and by the time they get to the coast, he is the one, and not his father, through whom revelation is coming about the construction of the boat.[46] The supplanting was complete by the time they got to the coast. When Lehi died in the new world, the parent connection was removed, the family lost their rallying point, and the older brothers' rebellion went into full swing. But the account omits what might have been a list of legitimate criticisms of

---

[44]   D&C 122:2.

[45]   See 2 Ne. 4:15–16.

[46]   1 Ne. 17:8.

Nephi by Laman and Lemuel, if we were able to hear their side of the story. We don't know what these criticisms were because we don't have any record of that. Nephi had no reason to include it.

But when it comes to the Prophet Joseph Smith, I do have that! You see, I not only have his autobiographical account, but I also have the written accounts of those who hated him. I have the written accounts of those who conspired to kill him. I do not have only the autobiographical material, as with Nephi. I have a wealth of information from many diverse sources about him.

I can still choose to be 'Lance entering the forest' in my approach to Joseph Smith. I can say I want to hear every word of criticism that anyone ever fabricated against the Prophet Joseph Smith, because it salves my conscience and it makes it easier for me to ignore what he restored. I needn't "awake" and I needn't "arise," and I needn't do anything about a message that may be authentic and comes from God, because I am able to find flaws in the messenger. But there is risk to that approach. I may be ignoring an authentic prophet who knew God, and was commissioned by Him to announce His message to me.

To return to the earlier questions: How important is it to look carefully at Joseph's words? How carefully should we consider what he left us? Is it enough to just take a superficial glance, trust others with institutional bias and motives? Do we need to show our gratitude and interest to God by looking as deeply as we can into his ministry? After all, he was among those who "knew more than [a person would] by reading everything that has ever been written on the subject" of heaven, because he had actually looked into it for himself.[47]

---

[47] "Could you gaze into heaven five minutes, you would know more than you would by reading all that ever was written on the subject." (*TPJS*, 324.)

When you have the unique opportunity to reckon the stature of a prophet from both those who loved him and those who hated him; from those who merely admire him, but are not converted, and can consider as well those who resented him; or who were one time converted by him but left his side, yet felt no need to turn violent toward him; you have a window available to you beyond anything comparable for another dispensation-opening prophet of God. When you have take mix of those various personalities, those various viewpoints converging on Joseph, to let you fully consider the meaning of the Prophet Joseph Smith's life, well then the more of that you can gather in one place, and consider, the greater your understanding becomes. You can measure the various reports in light of the motivations of the writers. You can see from them all a great deal more of Joseph's humanity and frailties, as well as his astounding strengths and power. Joseph Smith was not a deeply flawed human. Joseph Smith had a great deal about him that was altogether commendable. But he was too eager to take some people into his confidence, and he was often time misled by others because he attributed motives to them that reflected what his own inner motives were.

Unlike most people, I have the experiences in my life of having been hired to handle the problems of other people as their attorney. Because of these professional encounters, some of the shine has been taken off of the LDS business leader, the church leader, and the abusive spouse. I have seen too often that the fraudulent purveyor of a security scam whose entre' into the trust of his victim came because he was an LDS bishop or Stake President. Consequently I am unimpressed with office, social standing and religious reputation. It is conduct alone that matters. I taught a course at BYU Education Week on recognizing fraud during one of their Education Week cycles years ago. In it I suggested it was one of the "badges of fraud," and likely a scam, if the person who is trying to get you to invest tells you in the first 15 minutes about their religion and church calling. That is almost always an indicator they are trying to distract you into quick acceptance of their scheme. After all, the purpose behind the "sheep's clothing" always is to mislead. The only reason you don the clothing is because you hope that by appearing superficially to conform to a recognized image, you will be able to mislead and deceive. It is always the substance that matters. I do my best to avoid as much as possible the stereotypes of Mormonism. I do not want anyone to think I *should* be trusted. With anyone telling you truth, it is always the underlying message alone that matters. In general what matters is this: Does the message cause you to awake? Does it cause you to arise? Because we must be reminded relentlessly that the condition in which we find ourselves is one where it is absolutely necessary that you awake and arise, that you shake off the dust, and that you get out of the slumber in which you find yourself. There are those who have awakened only to find themselves in a nightmare of their own, making because the reaction to awakening is violent. Don't fear that. You will get over it. You will find God is eager to help once you've awakened. He has not left you here alone but will always comfort you.[48] In the proper circumstances and after your awakening has proceeded to the proper point, He will personally comfort you.[49] He will introduce you to the Father, also, and they will take up their abode with you, just as they did with Joseph Smith.[50]

I don't swim in the shallow end of the pool when it comes to Mormonism. The only end I have ever been in is the deep end. It

---

[48]   John 14:16.

[49]   John 14:18.

[50]   John 14:23

began when, indoctrinated by a Baptist mother, I sincerely believed the missionaries teaching me were out to perpetuate fraud. I had to overcome that to be converted to the faith. By overcoming that initial bias, and putting Mormonism to the test, I got an answer to prayer. There is no argument you can advance that will succeed in altering the reality that God answered my prayer. Therefore, when someone came to me after that point said to me, "Yeah, but they didn't tell you that Joseph Smith had wives! That is in the plural!" My reaction was, "Well, okay. I gotta look into that." Sure enough, there it was in section 132. But I suspended judgment on the entire plural marriage issue from the moment a critic tried to dissuade me from conversion, because I hadn't the time to really consider it. I have to tell you it was a real low priority for me. I thought it was weird, okay. I don't care if you are an advocate, and I don't even care if you practice it. You have to admit it's a weird arrangement. I love my wife. I don't want another one. In fact, my view is that the more you love your wife the less you want another one. The more delightful the relationship is, the less need there is to multiply complexity or try to find harmony among a larger group.

So when I first encountered this topic by someone hoping to deter me from becoming Mormon, I concluded, "if Joseph was going to take that on, then someday I will look into it and try to figure it." I suspended judgment on the issue, and I actually didn't reach closure on that topic until, maybe, four or five years ago. It just wasn't that important to figure it all out in a hurry. [Meaning that something of that sort cannot be decided correctly if you are in a rush—and not that the topic lacks importance. It is the haste which is improper.] I have reached closure on the issue, and you have the benefit of what I now think about it in the last book, *Passing the Heavenly Gift*. In there I explain my understanding of why Joseph practiced it. It is not what most folks suggest. I should add, I considered information from the polygamist community as part of the years of considering the topic. I also have read Ogden Kraut's information, though I have not yet finished reading all of his material. But hearing from those who believe intensely about the subject is something I felt I was required to do before reaching any conclusion on the matter.

There was news on this topic of Joseph Smith's plural wives while *Passing the Heavenly Gift* was still in manuscript form, and I could have added information about the recently concluded DNA testing. That is a study which has been updating through additional tests, and as a result there was another study in the news. The article was in the *Deseret News* on November 10, 2007.[51] We ought to be very open, we ought to be very fearless, about searching for truth. They have been trying to figure out all of the genetic markers that relate to Joseph Smith and his purported, prodigious, sexual exploits with the plural wives. Even as of a year and a half ago the last remaining trail that could have led to Joseph Smith having sired a child came to a dead end, and right now the only children conclusively Joseph Smith's are those children born to Emma Smith. That is it. We have that story about Eliza R Snow and that pregnancy, but even if you accept the account there was no progeny from that. You can put Eliza R. Snow on your list to investigate further, if you like. But, nevertheless, Joseph Smith fathered children only with Emma Smith.

Joseph Smith, as I walk through the topic in *Passing the Heavenly Gift*, got an answer to his inquiry concerning plural wives in 1829. It came to him as he was translating Jacob chapter 2 with Oliver Cowdery as scribe. This subject was just like the earlier encoun-

---

51   *DNA Tests Rule Out 2 as Smith Descendants: Scientific Advances Prove No Genetic Link*, which is available on-line.

ter with the topic of baptism during translating the book, which provoked him to inquire about the subject. As a result, John the Baptist appeared to him and both Joseph and Oliver were baptized. It was translating the Book of Mormon that was the trigger for the inquiry. He translated the Jacob 2 material and the topic of plural wives came up. This was during the year 1829.[52] And he got an answer to his inquiry. The answer informed him about the eternal marriage covenant first. Because when something provokes a person to inquire of the Lord, particularly when what they are inquiring about is something that really matters to them about which they would really like to get an answer, the answer usually contains at least two parts. In the one, the answer responds to the inquiry. In the other, the Lord tells mankind what matters to the Lord. This is often the case. The problem is a pretext, used by the Lord to drive the inquiry. And the answer to the inquiry includes much more than the subject about which the prophet inquires.

For example, in the case of the Brother of Jared, the inquiry was because they were struggling with an interior lighting problem in the barges then under construction.[53] That inquiry was used by the Lord as a convenient introduction to something which mattered

---

[52]   Now keep in mind he began with the record of Lehi abridged by Mormon, and he went all the way through 116 pages of translated text. At that point he entrusted Martin Harris and the 116 pages were lost. Joseph commenced the translation from the point it had stopped, after the 116 pages, till the end. When he got to the end, he was told to go back and use the small plates of Nephi and translate them to replace the missing 116 pages. So he translated the small plates of Nephi in which we find the text running from 1 Nephi to the Words of Mormon. The portion of the text in which the topic of plural wives is mentioned appears in Jacob, toward the end of the small plates of Nephi. So the translation raising of the topic is found in Jacob 2, and occurs very late in the process. The Book of Mormon was by that time all but finished. He still had the rest of Jacob, Enos, Jarom, Omni and the Words of Mormon left to do, but the work of translating was essentially complete by the point he inquires on the topic.

[53]   Ether 2:22.

a great deal more.[54] The Lord wanted to talk about redemption of Mahonri from the fall,[55] taking him back into His presence, and then give to him a plenary tour through the endowment, so he could understand the mysteries of God,[56] or in other words how everything in creation fits together. But the problem the man approached the Lord to solve was merely the practical problem of interior lighting.

Likewise Joseph approached the Lord about the topic of plural wives. But the answer he received began with another topic: the eternal marriage covenant. For that portion of the revelation, the information did not respond to Joseph's inquiry, and was limited to a single wife. You can read the first 28 verses, and the language revealing the eternal marriage covenant is always in the singular. It is "a wife" throughout.[57] The eternal marriage covenant is between a man and "a wife." After the portion of the revelation involving the eternal marriage covenant concludes, the Lord addressed the topic Joseph asked about. Beginning at verse 29 and going through 39 the answer to his question is given. For that, there are two specific and quite limited circumstances. I discuss all that in *Passing the Heavenly Gift* and won't repeat it again here.

Joseph dictated Section 132 on July 12, 1843 at Hyrum's request. Hyrum asked it be written down so he could take it to Emma and persuade her it was a true principle. Joseph Smith dictated the revelation July 12, 1843, but by that time much more had been received on the subject of eternal marriage and plural wives. As a result, when it was dictated he included not just the first answer, but

---

54   Ether Chapter 3.

55   Ether 3:13.

56   Ether 3:18.

57   See D&C 132:1-28.

also a series of revelations related to this topic, all the way down through events that were then unfolding in Nauvoo. There are at least 5 different revelations written into section 132, but there had been at least 6 revelations on the topic of plural marriage. One of those Joseph didn't bother putting into the text of Section 132. The one that is missing is one in which Joseph was commanded by an 'angel with a drawn sword' to take plural wives. He found the idea to be detestable. Joseph Smith complied after he had been told to comply by an angel who threatened him with being cut off. As I discuss in the book, Eliza R Snow's account of that I think is the correct one, the most accurate one. According to Sister Snow, he was told he would forfeit priesthood if he did not comply with the requirement. Therefore, Joseph complied. It was a dreadful ordeal for him, but he complied. Despite the omission of that information from Section 132, the results of Joseph's compliance are there. The Lord pronounced that Joseph had laid his heart on the altar and complied with what he was loath to do and would be rewarded for his sacrifice. The Lord confirmed to Joseph the knowledge of his calling and election, and restored to him the sealing power.[58] All of that happened before 1833, because Joseph uses the sealing power in 1833.[59]

Which leads us then to the topic I intend to write about here: I wanted to first remind you of this background before discussing The Mission of Elijah. Among the Latter-day Saints there is a narrative about Elijah which you are welcome to accept. I am going to explain in this only how I understand the topic. You are free to reject anything I have to say, and conclude the traditional narrative we have been handed is the right story. It is just like Alma said above,

---

[58]   D&C 132:45-50.

[59]   See D&C 88:1-5.

we can "take of the waters of life freely and whosoever does not come the same is not compelled to come." You don't need to come with me. You don't need to come with any man. You can be content as you are, and dismiss all I have to say as just my own suppositions. But I should add that I've made this a matter of study and inquiry, and therefore I think I am right. It is settled enough in my mind I feel comfortable writing about it now; and will bear testimony of it at the end. For me that is a serious matter.

Well, the story of Elijah actually began a long time ago. Joseph received a revelation stating that, "Three years previous to the death of Adam he called Seth, Enos, Cainan, Mahalaleel, Jared, Enoch and Methuselah who were all High Priests, with the residue of his posterity who were righteous, into the valley of Adam-ondi-Ahman, and there bestowed upon them his last blessing. And the Lord appeared unto *THEM*.[60] And they rose up and blessed Adam and called him Michael the Prince, the archangel. And the Lord administered comfort unto Adam, and said unto him, I have set thee to be at the head, a multitude of nations shall come of thee, and thou art a prince forever over them. And Adam stood up in the midst of the congregation and, notwithstanding he was bowed down with age, being full of the Holy Ghost predicted whatsoever should befall his posterity unto the latest generations. These things were all written in the book of Enoch." (D&C 107:53-57, emphasis added.) Enoch was one of the seven High Priests who were invited. By the way, the reference to "High Priests" in this account is not to the office we have in the church. In those days there was one, integrated priesthood. It was "after the Order of the Son of God."[61] There were no divisions and no offices, but a single integrated priesthood which

---

[60]   The reference to "them" is not to the entire group, but to the seven High Priests.

[61]   D&C 107:3.

possessed all the rights, including sealing authority, which comes with The Order of the Son of God. Later the priesthood was divided, separated, and limited. It wasn't that way in the beginning. In the beginning it was one. But with the passing of the various dispensations, and the limitations put on wicked men, priesthood got divided into three: Patriarchal, Melchizedek and Aaronic, including Levitical. In the church today, we have two of those.[62] That original, unified priesthood will return again, in the end of the world.[63]

Enoch was one of the seven High Priests who participated in that early meeting. So, here you have an interesting setting worth carefully thinking about. It takes place on the earth, three years previous to the death of Adam (927 years following the fall). There was a gathering in which there are seven priests who are qualified to stand before the Lord. And the Lord comes and appears unto *THEM*—that is the seven who hold this priesthood and Adam.[64] These seven who are present with Adam are direct lineal descendants of Adam, members of the same family.[65] Therefore, I would suspect they had all things in common among them. If the Lord came, even if only for this ceremonial moment, and dwelt among them, then this was Zion.

One of the participants in that moment on that day in that group was Enoch. It was Enoch also who recorded it. He testified of it in a book which we will, at some future point, be able to read.[66]

---

[62]   D&C 107:1.

[63]   Moses 6:7.

[64]   The "residue" of their righteous posterity were present. (D&C 107:53.) However, I read the appearance to "them" to be limited to the High Priests possessing the right to stand in the presence of God. (D&C 84:12—I also read "God, even the Father" in that verse (D&C 84:12) to mean Christ; see, e.g., Mormon 9:12; Ether 3:14; Mosiah 15:2-4.)

[65]   The account is priesthood only, not genealogy!

[66]   D&C 107:57.

Here we have a brief moment in man's history which fits the definition of Zion. It is diminutive, and it is temporary, and it is tightly confined to a narrow group.[67] But we should take notice of it. It is not a thundering congregation of 3.7 million Temple Recommend holders all crowding about. It isn't a crowd at all. It is instead a very small group. But it is a group with whom it is possible for the Lord to come and dwell. Among their number is Enoch. So we see Enoch with the fathers learned the pattern for Zion, even if his city would not be translated from this earth for hundreds of years still in the future. He saw what was possible for his people in a meeting held three years previous to the death of Adam. Once he saw the pattern, it was his (and now our) duty to work to repeat it, to teach it, to bring it about.[68]

If you want the criteria or the description of Zion, you can read it in the Book of Moses. In Moses 7:16 we find this description: "From that time forth there were wars and bloodshed among them. But the Lord came and dwelt with his people and they dwelt in righteousness." This is an interesting contrast. Here you have wars and bloodshed on the one hand, but then you have the Lord dwelling among people, who are living in peace and righteousness on the other hand. "The fear of the Lord was upon all nations so great was the glory of the Lord it was upon his people." (*Id.* v. 17.) It was the "glory of the Lord upon his people" that intimidated the wicked. The Lord doesn't show Himself to the wicked except to destruc-

---

67   The "residue" who were present were blessed to be there, but as I read the verse the direct participants who were in the presence of the Lord was confined to Adam and the seven High Priests, one from each generation from Adam, Enoch being the seventh.

68   This is not unlike Joseph Smith conducting Zion's Camp, which Brigham Young observed. Later, when faced with the exodus from Nauvoo, Brigham mimicked Joseph's organization and propounded "The Word and Will of the Lord" which is now Section 136 of the Doctrine & Covenants. It was, in Brigham's mind, the Lord's will to repeat the pattern Joseph showed them earlier.

tion, but the Lord shows Himself unto those who are prepared. The "glory of the Lord upon them" is what others find intimidating.[69] And that was the case with these people of Enoch's Zion.

"And the Lord blessed the land and they were blessed upon the mountains and upon the high places and did flourish." (Moses 7:17.) That is literal, by the way. Zion was not located in a valley, either in the past or in the future. Zion belongs on a high place. Read the prophecies and you will note that to be true. I'm not going to walk through that here. "And the Lord called his people Zion because they were of one heart and one mind, dwelt in righteousness, and there were no poor among them." (*Id.* v. 18.) Of these, the words "and the Lord dwelt among them" are the most important. But He could not do so unless they were united. Becoming one and rising up to receive the proper order of things is but a prelude to the Lord's presence. For us, this poses a socio-economic problem, because we do not think it is even wise to attempt to have no poor among us. We think people prosper according to their genius, and therefore have earned all they have; or correspondingly, deserve all they lack.[70] When you are a family, as the original Zion, those competitive ideas are not even entertained.

We need to understand Enoch, because he is important for us to be able to understand Elijah. Again, I am only explaining my understanding of the relevance of Elijah. I want to be clear this is not the same story other Latter-day Saints tell concerning Elijah. You are free to accept what other folks say because, well, who am I? I'm just another Mormon with my own opinion, and nothing more.

---

[69]   See, e.g., Exo. 34:34-35.

[70]   This is the anti-Christ Korihor's doctrine. See Alma 30:17.

So, we have Enoch present at the first Zion (D&C 107:48). Enoch was 25 years old when he was ordained under the hand of Adam. Then he was 65 when "Adam blessed him." That ought to tell you something right there. In *Passing the Heavenly Gift* I suggest it is useful to view ordination as only an invitation. The invitation given through ordination is authoritative and available through The Church of Jesus Christ of Latter Day Saints. You should not expect to get an invitation through ordination elsewhere.[71]

However, an ordination or invitation is not the same thing as receiving the power of the priesthood. When you walk through the lives of all these priestly men, you see there is a two-fold event. First is an ordination. Then later there is empowerment or ratification of the ordination by heaven. Ordination involves men. Empowerment involves the heavens.[72] In the case of Nephi's brother Jacob, who was ordained by Nephi, we see the pattern set out. Jacob explains about his ordination by his brother,[73] and then later confirms, he "first obtained mine errand from the Lord." (Jacob 1:17.) There is a difference between the invite extended through ordination, and the blessing that comes when the power is conferred by heaven. You can see that dichotomy again in the case of Enoch, because Enoch was 25 years old when he was ordained by the hand of Adam, and forty years later he was 65 when Adam blessed him. Once the power came, "he saw the Lord, and he walked with him, and was before his face continually; and he walked with God 365 years making him 430 years old and he was translated." (D&C 107:49.) So, he

---

71   The only limit on that would involve John the Beloved or the Three Nephites, or the other angels mentioned in D&C 77:11. I discussed these other sources of priestly power in *Beloved Enos*, and it is beyond the scope of this essay, so it will not be repeated again here.

72   See D&C 121:36. This is why priesthood power is so rare a commodity, appearing only infrequently on the earth.

73   See 2 Ne. 6:2.

is ordained (the first requirement), then he is blessed (the second part), which has the effect of him becoming "continually before the Lord" (the intended result of ordination). We pick up the story once again in Moses 6:25: "And Enoch lived 65 years and begat Methuselah." Enoch had been ordained to the priesthood, but was not a father until he was "blessed" and entered the Lord's presence. These little details matter. Having a wife and being able to ascend to the Lord's presence are not unrelated.[74] They are, instead, intimately connected. They matter more than you can possibly imagine unless you comprehend the Gospel of Christ. There is something coincidental with Enoch becoming approved by the Lord and Enoch becoming completed as a person; because there is neither the man without the woman separately in the Lord.[75] They are both together. Therefore the narrative we are reading assumes you might know something about the Gospel, and assumes when you see this that you will take note of it. It just presupposes you understand that man cannot be saved separately and singly.[76] Man is saved in a union designed, like God, to produce progeny. Without the woman there is no salvation for man. There is no happiness without the woman, and when you manage to cajole, intimidate, berate and belittle a spouse to obtain from her (or him) reluctant submission, you haven't produced anything worthy of eternal preservation. You haven't produced anything that God will take note of and say, "Hey! This looks like Heaven." Let's hold on to this for all eternity. Because this is an environment inside which we can produce progeny and they will grow up to inherit worthy opportunities from their parents."

---

[74]   Man is not completed until married. But marriage is not completed until an enduring relationship exists.

[75]   1 Cor. 11:11.

[76]   See D&C 132:15-17.

If you have read the "Tenth Parable,"[77] you will recall the thing which caused the stirring to begin among the angels was something on earth that looked like Heaven. There was a man and a woman whose experience and circumstances mirrored the same kind of things that the angels, who are always watching, recognized from where they reside. They got the Lord, and He came and evaluated, concluding to save this union into eternity. He gave the angels a "to do list" for the preservation of the couple; hence the title of the parable. The angels then got busy with the assignment, and eighteen years later there was fruit worthy of storing in the Lord's storehouse.[78]

Returning to the record in the Book of Moses, Enoch had fathered a child and "Enoch journeyed in the land among the people, and as he journeyed the spirit of God descended out of Heaven and abode upon him; and he heard a voice from heaven, saying: Enoch, my son, prophecy unto this people." (Moses 6:27.) It goes by real quick, but in this verse God just took Fatherhood over Enoch as His son. You ought to note that because that means something too. "Enoch, my son," because Enoch has arrived in the place which priesthood is intended to bring him. The direction given to Enoch by God is this: "prophesy unto this people, and say unto them—Repent, for thus saith the Lord: I am angry with this people and my fierce anger is kindled against them for their hearts have waxed hard, and their ears are dull of hearing, and their eyes cannot see afar off. And for these many generations, since the day that I created them, they have gone astray, and have denied me, and have sought their own counsels in the dark; and in their own abominations have they devised murder, and have not kept the

---

[77]   *The Missing Virtue*, found in *Ten Parables*.

[78]   See Jacob 5:74.

commandments, which I have given unto the father, Adam." (Moses 6:27-28.) As soon as Enoch is restored to God's bosom, to the abode of the Father, to fellowship with the Church of the First-born, or in other words, when he receives power in his priesthood; immediately he receives a commission to cry repentance. His message, like the message of any true prophet, is for man to repent. Because there won't be a single soul saved if that soul does not repent and return to God.

"And when Enoch had heard these words, he bowed himself to the earth, before the Lord, and spake before the Lord, saying: Why is it that I have found favor in thy sight, and am but a lad, and all the people hate me; for I am slow of speech; [that doesn't mean what you think it means] wherefore am I thy servant?" This comment about being "slow of speech" does not mean he is inarticulate or somehow impaired. He is not at all "slow" as we use the word. He was a brilliant man. He was an articulate man. He was a most capable man. He wrote the record which Moses preserved in his account, and Joseph Smith restored to us by revelation. He is always envisioned anciently as the Great Scribe. To the Egyptians he is Thoth, the Scribe, the one who brings wisdom, who brought knowledge. So this phrase probably means something else.

He is "slow of speech," quite frankly, because he would rather think about it than talk about it. He would rather consider a matter carefully than speak quickly about it. He would rather be left alone than to make public declarations. He would rather have his privacy, his family, and a few close intimate friends, than he would to minister to people who don't give a damn about what he has to say. He would have preferred to avoid contact with those who think he is a wild man come among them,[79] because they believe he has no busi-

---

[79]   Moses 6:38.

ness delivering the message. He was trusted by the Lord precisely because the message was the Lord's and Enoch would not add to it because he craved attention. In other words, being "slow of speech" is a qualifier, not a handicap, for Enoch as the Lord's messenger.

Well, the Lord wouldn't take Enoch's reluctance. He told Enoch: "Go forth, do as I have commanded." (*Id.* v. 32.) The Lord says, "Open thy mouth, and it shall be filled, and I will give thee utterance, for all flesh is in my hands, and I will do as seemeth me good. Say unto this people: Choose ye this day, to serve the Lord God who made you. Behold my Spirit is upon you, wherefore all thy words will I justify." (*Id.* vs. 32-34.)

Enoch is told at this point though he was a person who was "slow of speech," or in other words a reluctant draftee, that the mountains will flee before him and the rivers will turn their course and Enoch will abide in the Lord and the Lord will abide in Enoch.[80] A person who is "quick of speech" given the power to speak and alter the location of mountains and rivers is completely unqualified to receive the power. They must be "slow of speech" or, in other words, must be willing to proceed meekly, with long suffering, with kindness, gentleness and unfeigned love as they minister in the priesthood.[81] This is always the case. Therefore only few ever receive priesthood power from God.[82]

These things happen to Enoch when he was 65 years old. But it would be some several hundred years later before the word of Enoch has the effect the Lord promised Enoch at this point. The Lord has all things in front of Him, and therefore could see where

---

[80]   Moses 6:34.

[81]   See D&C 121:41-42.

[82]   D&C 121:40.

this was going.[83] But Enoch, who is down here in this fallen world, although a seer,[84] has not developed to this point yet. What the Lord gave to Enoch is not akin to "pixie dust." These great gifts of the Spirit are always acquired in exactly the same way, in every generation when they appear, by everyone who acquires them. It is always through the exercise of each person's faith. The way in which people exercise their faith is always by conforming their outward actions to their innermost true beliefs, even when the actions taken are difficult. Even when the Lord asks of you something you are very reluctant to place upon the altar. Even when everyone will hate you for what it is you do. Nevertheless, Enoch did what he was asked. We haven't time to fully discuss Enoch's ministry and I wouldn't want to rob you of the joy of discovering for yourself what great things then unfolded. It is covered there in Moses Chapter 6, but we are going to have to move on.

I do want to take note the Lord gave to Enoch a description of the Holy Ghost. That description is found in Moses 6:61: "Therefore it is given to abide in you; the record of heaven; the Comforter; the peaceable things of immortal glory; the truth of all things; that which quickeneth all things, which maketh alive all things; that which knoweth all things, and hath all power according to wisdom, mercy, truth, justice, and judgment." That is the definition of the Holy Ghost. On the list was the word "Comforter." It is the definition that Jesus will endorse later.[85] I don't know if He had the record of Enoch in front of Him when He made that endorsement. But it was Jesus speaking to Enoch at the time this revelation was given, and the "Comforter" shows up as a common descriptor.

---

[83]   D&C 130:7.

[84]   Moses 6:36.

[85]   John 14:16-17.

If you take verse 61 as the definition of the Holy Ghost, then the Holy Ghost is the "record of Heaven." The Holy Ghost is the "Comforter." The Holy Ghost is "the peaceable things of immortal glory." The Holy Ghost is "the truth of all things." The Holy Ghost is "that which quickeneth all things which maketh alive all things." The Holy Ghost is "that which knoweth all things and hath all power according to wisdom, mercy, truth, justice, and judgment." You will get a lot closer to understanding about why it is that the Holy Ghost is a "personage of spirit that dwelleth within you" and is not a personage of tabernacle because otherwise it could not "dwell within you"[86] and other such interesting things, if you consider carefully the definition of the Holy Ghost given by the Lord to Enoch in this verse.

Well, Enoch launched his ministry, cried repentance to his generation, and at some point in his ministry he did accomplish what the Lord said he would some hundreds of years earlier. Skipping forward to Moses 7:13 we read: "And so great was the faith of Enoch that he led the people of God, and their enemies came to battle against them; and he spake the word of the Lord, and the earth trembled, and the mountains fled, even according to his command; and the rivers of water were turned out of their course; and the roar of the lions was heard out of the wilderness; and all nations feared greatly, so powerful was the word of Enoch, and so great was the power of the language which God had given him." This is also one of the unique attributes about Zion. When you have Zion in place, then it is the Lord who fights the battles for them.[87] You will not need to have a weapon's budget in Zion's camp. It doesn't happen that way. The battle to be fought is fought by the

---

[86]   D&C 130:22.

[87]   See, e.g., D&C 45:67; 64:43; 49:27; 3 Ne. 20:42; 21:29.

Lord. The prophecy given through Joseph Smith about the last days predicts the wicked decide they will not take on Zion, because Zion will be too terrible. They will reach that conclusion entirely because of the presence of the Lord there.[88] It is not because of munitions. In fact, that same description includes a statement about Zion's residents. They are those who will *not* take up arms against their neighbor, but instead flee to Zion. They are the only ones that aren't killing others.[89]

Which then begs the question: Why is the remnant that will build Zion also going to "tear in pieces and trample under foot" the gentiles?[90] Why, or how do they do that? You must stop thinking of Zion as a bunch of action film heroes, a Rambo with a howitzer in his hand, and instead start thinking about the image of Babylon to be torn in pieces and be trodden under foot.[91] You do not need anything other than the truth to tear in pieces the Gentile's false kingdoms. And I can assure you, it will all be trodden under foot by the truth. All that is needed is the truth proclaimed by someone sent by Him, then rejected by those claiming they are God's chosen, saved people, and the Lord will bring the entire Gentile idol down to ashes. Then it will be trodden under foot.

Zion's final development in Enoch's day is described in these words: "The fear of the Lord was upon all nations, so great was the glory of the Lord, which was upon his people. And the Lord blessed the land, and they were blessed upon the mountains, and upon the high places, and did flourish." (Moses 7:17.) That is where you will find Zion in Enoch's day. Not on a plain and not in a valley.

---

[88]   D&C 45:67.

[89]   *Id.*, v. 68.

[90]   See Christ's description in 3 Ne. 16:8, 15.

[91]   Daniel 2:44-45.

You will find it in the high places on the mount. Not merely symbolically. No one will have a height from which to overlook into the goings-on of Zion. They will be beneath, and Zion will be above. And Zion's presence will be terrible. For the wicked, it will be as the same problem Israel had before the mountain, when Moses was upon the mountain communing with the Lord.[92]

Mountaintops, as we all know, are acceptable substitutes for temples. I doubt the kind of people who initially build Zion in any day have had, or are going to have, the means with which to build what needs to be built. It is of no concern, however, because the Lord has a way of making due. "The Lord called his people Zion, because they were of one heart, and one mind, and dwelt in righteousness; and there was no poor among them." (Moses 7:18.) There were no poor among them physically; there were no poor among them spiritually. They did not compete, they cooperated. Then did not envy, they shared. They did not pass a zoning law.

I will tell you how to ruin Zion, how to keep it from coming: Pass a zoning law. Decide you're going to 'police the neighborhood.' Start thinking you should have restrictive covenants, so you can enforce views upon one another. The instant you start to regulate one another, Zion it is gone. It slips right between your fingers. No man needs to say to another: 'know ye the Lord; for they all are going to know him who dwell in Zion.' The new song to be sung presupposes the residents of Zion will know the Lord.[93]

I thought about writing a fictional account of this curious city in which those people who have several children live in big houses, while those who have no children live in small houses. In the place,

---

[92]   See Exo. 20:18-21 for a description of how the unworthy react to God's appearance. See Mormon 9:2-5 for the reason for this reaction.

[93]   See D&C 84:98-102.

no one has a job or schedule, but everyone works. One day the lead character gets up, walks outside, and notices that the lawn needs to be mowed. So he goes and finds a lawn mower and starts mowing. He mows at his house, then the next, then finds he has spent days mowing grass and is across the city to the other side. Everywhere he has been he found grass needing mowing, and he took care of it. He finishes after a couple of weeks, then returns to his house and says, "Hey, look at that; the grass has grown again." So he starts mowing again. He does this because he feels like mowing the grass at the time. He just wants to.

Then after the season, he notices there is only one person working in the local bakery. He had never worked in a bakery, but he decides to go see what it is like to work in a bakery—and he rather likes that. So he spends the next seasons in the bakery doing that. The following year he wonders whatever happened to the lawns. They have been cut since the new Spring, but he doesn't know who has been cutting them. He goes on his way to find out who has been cutting the yard, because he liked doing that, he has something in common with whoever is now mowing the grass. He would like to know how they like it and what their pattern for taking care of the work has become. He wants to ask them: "How did you do that?" But on his way, he gets distracted by the orchard needing harvesting, so he spends that Fall harvesting there.

So the story just ends, with what appears to be total chaos. A completely ungoverned society, in which oddly enough everyone is at peace, but no one is in control. No one has a job, but everyone works; and the only thing that motivates any resident is what needs to be done: "Hey, let's take care of this" is the only motivation. And they do it for as long as they feel like doing it, and then they do something else. It is a story I've considered writing, but have never done so. But now the idea for the story is in this essay, so you can write it in your own mind.

Our vision of Zion is regimented, regulated. We're Mormons after all! We want to be controlled. A man cannot be saved unless there's a boss at the top. "This is your assignment." "We are going to call you, we are going to sustain you." "We are going to put your conscripted ass in this position and park it there and you must *magnify* that job!"—I am not sure anyone knows what "magnify" means, but I tell you, you better be calling attention to yourself so that everyone notices because, we can't have the invisible lawn mower. We can't have the invisible baker. We can't have the invisible in harmony with everyone around them harvesting the orchard when it needs doing. Because this is the Zion Reich!—As soon as you do that, it is gone. It has slipped between your fingers. Zion is without compulsion.[94] Zion will occur when the Lord brings again Zion.[95] And it will happen perfectly naturally. But only among those who are fit to participate.

But we have to move on because we are trying to figure out what role Elijah occupies in this return of Zion.

Continuing in Moses 7:20-21, 23: "And it came to pass that Enoch talked with the Lord; and he said unto the Lord: Surely Zion shall dwell in safety forever. But the Lord said unto Enoch: Zion have I blessed, but the residue of the people have I cursed. And it came to pass that the Lord showed unto Enoch all the inhabitants of the earth; and he beheld, and lo, Zion, in process of time, was taken up into heaven....And after that Zion was taken up into heaven, Enoch beheld, and lo, all the nations of the earth were be-

---

[94]   D&C 121:46.

[95]   See 3 Nephi 16:18, Isaiah 52:8.

fore him;" and so on. Enoch and his city depart. Zion existed, then it was taken to heaven and fled from this earth. Zion really never belongs here, you see. When it comes, the Lord dwells among them, and in the process of time the city is taken to heaven. At least that was the case in the past. In the future, it will be established to throw down the kingdoms of this world and displace them.

We have looked at two examples: one from Section 107, and this one from the Book of Moses involving Enoch. Remember Enoch was there at the earlier event described in Section 107. These two moments of Zion have Enoch in common between them. But they also have two other things in common: They were one—united and in harmony with one another. And the Lord came and dwelt among them. Those are all essential for Zion.

Well, so Enoch and his city were taken up. Enoch's son and Noah's father, Methuselah, remained behind and the story continues.[96] Before continuing, however, let me remind you again I am offering you my view. I am not offering you something which has been endorsed recently, although tit was one time believed among the Latter-day Saints. This idea has been denounced by Elder Bruce R. McConkie. In any event, it is my view that Melchizedek was the new name given to Shem.[97] And Shem is, of course the son of Noah. When it is talking about the priesthood through the fa-

---

[96]   Moses 8:2. This verse discloses that God covenanted with Enoch to leave his son, Methuselah behind to make Noah a descendant of Enoch's. This resulted in the second father of mankind, Noah, being the grandson of Enoch. All mankind thereafter would reckon Enoch as one of their "fathers" through whom we all descend.

[97] John Taylor declared Shem to be Melchizedek in the December 15, 1844 *Times and Seasons,* Vol. 5, p. 746.

ther's unto Noah[98] as the basis for a doctrinal interpretation[99] I do not believe that means there were generations separating Noah from Melchizedek. That is not how I read the verse. I read it to mean "through the fathers from Adam down to Noah." I think the connection between Noah and Melchizedek was immediate, father and son, Noah the father and Shem the son. If that is correct, the connection between Enoch's Zion and Melchizedek's City of Peace is much more direct. There is a connection between the two. Shem was an adult when he entered the Ark with his family. He would have known of his great-grandfather, Enoch and his city. These initial appearances of Zion in this world are connected because the first one, in the valley of Adam-ondi-Ahman, occurs while Enoch is present. The second one occurs with Enoch in a city he established and taught for 365 years.[100] The third was with Shem, Enoch's great-grandson, who would have known a great deal concerning his fathers, if Shem is in fact Melchizedek.

The third Zion occurred when Melchizedek, who was acquainted with those earlier patriarchs who lived on the other side of the flood, established his City of Peace. Melchizedek or Shem was an adult when he enter the ark. He knew of Enoch and the options

---

[98]   D&C 84:14.

[99]   Bruce R. McConkie, for example, taught: "There is an unsupported tradition to the effect that Melchizedek was the same person as Shem the son of Noah. That this could hardly have been the case is seen from the revelation which says: "Abraham received the priesthood from Melchizedek, who received it *through the lineage of his fathers, even till Noah*." (D. & C. 84:14.) In other words, there seem to have been at least two generations between Melchizedek and Shem." (*Mormon Doctrine*, 475.) But Deseret Book has just discontinued printing *Mormon Doctrine*. So perhaps Elder McConkie's views will be less important to the Saints in the future.

[100]   Moses 7:68.

presented to mankind through Enoch. They would either be taken into heaven, or they would have to board the Ark.[101]

At that moment in history God was going to destroy the world. But a dilemma arises because a group living in the world had attained the status of Zion. Since they are in a state of being Zion, the world could not destroy them.[102] It is fair game for the wicked to destroy the righteous. The wicked are allowed to destroy the righteous all the time in history. If you don't believe that then go ask Amulek, who suggested to Alma they stretch forth their hands and use the power of God to stop the killing of innocent believers.[103] Alma rejected the idea saying "the Lord receiveth them up unto himself, in glory; and he doth suffer that they may do this thing, or that the people may do this thing unto them, according to the hardness of their hearts, that the judgments which he shall exercise upon them in his wrath may be just." (Alma 14:11.) These people are received up into glory. These people who are righteous are slain this way because the wicked get to kill them. They get to kill them because God will judge the wicked by taking their lives. That is the system. God can slay the wicked, but God cannot slay the righteous. The wicked kill the righteous.

The most righteous man who ever lived was allowed to be killed by the wicked. In fact, it was indispensible for the wicked to kill Him, because otherwise there could not have been an atonement made. Therefore, Christ was slain at the hands of wicked men. But there is always a problem when it comes to Zion. The wicked cannot destroy it, and God cannot do so, because it is contrary to the

---

[101]   Being "caught up...into Zion" continued even after Enoch ascended and until the time of the flood. (See Moses 7:27.)

[102]   Moses 7:17.

[103]   Alma 14:10.

justice of God to do the killing. So what does God do to solve this dilemma? Well, what was introduced was a new status for a portion of humanity. That new status is to take them into heaven and translate them into a new condition above the status of mortality on this earth. But the Lord did not (perhaps could not) take people into heaven without giving them an associated calling to justify taking them. There is no reason ever to take a person off the earth, even if they are righteous, unless there is some calling to justify it. Abraham was the father of the righteous, yet he died and was buried. Christ died, and He was more righteous than anyone that ever lived. But He died and was buried. Though He rose again the third day, yet He was not spared death by being translated. God does not take any man off the earth through translating them unless they have a calling to minister. So, the City of Enoch received a calling to minister to others. They were given 2 callings: Their first assignment is as ministering angels,[104] not only here but elsewhere to other people.[105] The second calling (and I don't want to appear irreverent in saying this), but they are the cheering group backing up the Lord at His Second Coming. They are the ones when He comes in the clouds with his angels, that group will include Enoch's and Melchizedek's people.[106] They are the certifiers, they are the testifiers, they are the chorus, they are the entourage.

There is a reason why our tin-horn dictators, and our phony idols have an entourage. It is to mimic the real deal, because when the Lord comes again in His glory, He is going to come with an entourage. The pretenders mimic the real thing. Oddly they are "inspired" to do so, because somewhere deep within we all know the

---

[104]   D&C 130:5.

[105]   See *TPJS* 170.

[106]   Jude 1:14.

Lord has His "hosts" who come with Him. So we reenact some-thing Divine, without even knowing it testifies of Christ.

To save Enoch's City, they got the calling to minister and ac-company the Lord at His return. Melchizedek, who was acquainted with his great-grandfather Enoch's conditions, in my view, was nec-essarily offered the same option by the Lord.[107] Melchizedek should have been able to be "caught up...unto Zion" as well. But he also had the option to remain and enter the Ark. Noah was also qualified to leave, but was asked to remain. All of those who were saved on the Ark were aware of the possibility of translation into Enoch's Zion,[108] perhaps excepting only Ham's wife, Egyptus.[109]

It seems like a reasonable request by Melchizedek to be permit-ted, at the end of his mortal sojourn, to join Enoch. After he fin-ished his ministry following the Flood, he should have been given the option to also take qualified people with him into heaven, just as Enoch had done before.

In the course of time, Melchizedek established a city, a City of Peace, a city of righteousness. He was a king and a priest, and he presided over his people in righteousness.[110] You should read the word "presided" as "taught" rather than a strong-man.[111] Abraham, who was converted to the truth, came to Melchizedek and paid

---

[107] See Moses 7:27.

[108] *Id.*

[109] See Moses 7:22; Abraham 1:22-23.

[110] JST-Gen. 14:36.

[111] Throughout the competition between Nephi and the older brothers, the word "ruler" is synonymous with "teacher" over them. See, e.g., 1 Ne. 2:22; 2 Ne. 5:19. When, therefore, a pretended "ruler" spends his time controlling and dominating others, but fails to teach them in the path of righteousness, he fails to qualify as a "ruler" and has abdicated his position before God.

tithes.[112] They had a ceremonial get-together, which among other things included a sacral meal.[113] Melchizedek, who has been waiting for this moment, 'hands the football' to Abraham (or in other words appoints the new presiding High Priest), and says, in effect: "At last! Me and my people are gone!"[114] So, once again Zion flees.

Notice, if you will, that the Priesthood after the Order of the Son of God has been renamed the Priesthood of Enoch,[115] and then renamed again the Melchizedek Priesthood.[116] The reason for renaming the priesthood was because these priests established Zion, took people into heaven, and were Preachers of Righteousness.

For Melchizedek we have an extended explanation of him in the Joseph Smith Translation of the Bible, in Genesis Chapter 14, beginning with verse 25:

"And Melchizedek lifted up his voice and blessed Abram. Now Melchizedek was a man of faith, who wrought righteousness; and when a child he feared God, and stopped the mouths of lions, and quenched the violence of fire. And thus, having been approved of God, he was ordained an high priest after the order of the covenant which God made with Enoch," (vs. 25-27.) He's got the same covenant as had been previously made with Enoch. He possesses the same, single High Priesthood which was in the beginning. When there was only one, and not three, orders, Melchizedek is one of those who held this Holy Order and High Priesthood. Continuing,

---

[112] JST-Gen. 14:36-39.

[113] Gen. 14:18-19.

[114] See JST-Gen. 14:32. I am, of course, converting the dialogue into modern language. There was a complete sense of relief and fulfillment when Abraham arrived and the city could move up.

[115] D&C 76:57.

[116] D&C 107:3.

"It being after the order of the Son of God; which order came, not by man, nor the will of man; neither by father nor mother; neither by beginning of days nor end of years; but of God; And it was delivered unto men by the calling of his own voice, according to his own will, unto as many as believed on his name." (vs. 28-29.)

This is how this priesthood is delivered. It is given by God's "own voice" calling to the man. Joseph Smith tells us when he got this Melchizedek Priesthood, in my view. And in my view (which is not the view taught in church), it did not involve Peter James and John. I think they, like others, delivered keys to Joseph. But Melchizedek Priesthood came to Joseph the same as it came to Melchizedek and the same as it is delivered to anyone: "by the calling of [God's] own voice" as the verse above states. Joseph said he received it through "the voice of God in the chamber of old Father Whitmer, in Fayete, Seneca county." (D&C 128:21.) I am persuaded that Peter James and John like other angelic ministers came to deliver keys, but not Melchizedek Priesthood because the priesthood of Melchizedek comes only from God's own voice. Joseph knew this, of course, because he translated the above verses of the Joseph Smith Translation of Genesis Chapter 14. Just as was done anciently, "it was delivered unto [Joseph Smith] by the calling of [God's] own voice, according to his own will." We can ordain people all day long, but the manner in which the ordination assumes power is through "the calling of God's own voice." That's the description given by the Prophet Joseph Smith in the translation of Genesis 14. Joseph mentions that event took place from the voice of God to him in the chamber of old Father Whitmer, as set out in his letter now found in D&C 128:21.[117]

As an aside, D&C 128 is a letter Joseph Smith wrote in Nauvoo. It is late in his ministry. He wrote it while in hiding in Nauvoo. He was trying to stay in contact with the Saints. I make no reference to this in *Passing the Heavenly Gift*, but it is another example, just as it is a glaring omission from the last testimony of Oliver Cowdery, that Joseph also makes no mention of Elijah's appearance in his letter (now Section 128). In the list of the angelic ministrants who came to Joseph Smith in his letter composed in 1842, six years *after* the appearance of Elijah in the Kirtland Temple, Elijah is not mentioned. Likewise, throughout the Nauvoo time period up to 1844, Joseph refers to Elijah's coming as a future, not a past, event. If the return of Elijah is a still future event in 1842, 1843, and 1844, then the appearance of Elijah in the Kirtland Temple cannot fulfill the promised mission of Elijah.

But we are ahead of the story. Let's go back to the ministry of the man called Melchizedek for a moment. In his case, once again, we see a repetition of the pattern in which there is a prophet-minister as well as a people who respond to the message of repentance. The people left their wickedness and established a City of Peace,[118] in which the Lord could come to dwell with them.[119] In both Enoch's and Melchizedek's cities, when they obtain this condi-

---

[117] There is an essay written by Andrew F. Ehat on this topic. He writes about the difference between conferral of Melchizedek Priesthood, by God's voice, and a subsequent visit by Peter, James and John to deliver keys. See *The Joseph Smith 1839 Account of Restoration of the Melchizedek Priesthood: A Personal Essay*. The "voice of God in the chamber of old Father Whitmer" is the source of the priesthood that made Joseph and Oliver apostles, as referred to in Section 18 of the Doctrine and Covenants.

[118] JST-Gen. 14:36.

[119] *Id.* v. 34.

tion they are taken up into heaven. Zion, in the form of these cities taken into heaven, evaporates from the scriptural record after that.

We do have the Neophyte experience, where the Lord came and He dwelt among them.[120] The corridor was opened and the Lord, as well as angels, descended to them.[121] But they were not taken up into heaven through the ascent, and for a moment I want to stay on the idea of Zion's ascent up the heavenly corridor. The Nephite experience, just like the first Zion with Adam, resulted in the righteous living to old age and then dying, rather than being removed into heaven. All of those with Adam died, except Enoch and his people. Enoch's people did not die, but were instead taken up to heaven. And then Melchizedek and his city was likewise taken up into heaven. In all the subsequent experiences when the Lord visited with people, whether it is in Jerusalem, or whether it is in the new world, it never again resulted in Zion ascending into heaven. That didn't happen. But there are other incidents which occurred, involving individuals who made the ascent. Moses was taken up into heaven. The last person to make the ascent was Elijah.[122] Let's turn to some of what the record tells us about the ministry of Elijah.

Elijah is an interesting fellow. He raised someone from the dead,[123] he helped the widow of Zarephath whom he miraculously saved through a drought,[124] and he went upon the mountain to be taught by the Lord. On the mountain he encountered the Lord, who told him the way in which he can recognize the voice of God for-

---

[120]   See 3 Nephi beginning with Chapter 11.

[121]   See 3 Nephi 11:8; 17:24.

[122]   See 2 Kings 2:11.

[123]   1 Kings 17:17-22.

[124]   1 Kings 17:9-16.

ever thereafter.[125] He confronted the priests of Baal, and called down fire from heaven.[126] This last incident was rather a remarkable demonstration. Before calling fire down, he had water dumped all over the altar of twelve stones, until a trench around the altar was filled with water.[127] Then he called down fire from heaven, which consumed the sacrifice, the water and the altar itself.[128] He then killed 450 prophets of Baal, and 400 prophets of the groves.[129] All of this going on rather testifies Elijah is now in possession of some of the power and spirit of God that belonged to Enoch's and Melchizedek's order.[130] In his career he developed to the point he became quite adept at its use, so much so that he stopped being inhibited about public displays.

Well, the moment came when Elijah was going to leave. It is interesting because his coming departure was not kept secret. When Elisha and Elijah were on their way to the place at which Elijah was going to be taken up into heaven, as they were going along there were folks (also called "prophets") who said, in effect, "Hey, Elisha you are loosing Elijah today. This is the day he is going."[131] It was not a secret it was going to happen. So, Elijah was on his way and Elisha was with him, and Elisha wanted to know if he could obtain the same priesthood. He asked: "I pray thee, let a double portion of thy spirit be upon me."[132] Elijah, recognized this is not a connection

[125] 1 Kings 19:11-12.

[126] 1 Kings 18:18-40.

[127] *Id.* vs. 33-35.

[128] *Id.* vs. 37-39.

[129] *Id.* vs. 20, 40.

[130] See JST Gen. 14:30-32.

[131] See 2 Kings 2:3-7.

[132] *Id.* v. 9.

which men form among men, but this authority comes from and requires a connection to heaven. Therefore he told Elisha, "it is a hard thing" to accomplish this. However, if Elisha was there when the corridor opens and the fiery ascent was shown to him, Elisha would have this priesthood conferred by heaven upon him.[133] This was because when the heavens open the presence of God is always there. And a person cannot behold such things without possessing this priesthood.[134] The witness, if he was there, will have the power conferred upon him to stand in the presence of God and live. Elisha was told, in effect, "if you witness it, it will be yours to know and have." Elisha was in fact with him when he was taken up.[135] In a sign of benevolence and charity, Elijah cast his mantle down and Elisha picked it up.[136] Then as Elisha returned from the ascent of Elijah, as he got to the river Jordan he struck it with the mantle, and the river stopped and he walked over on dry ground.[137] Elisha then knew this priestly power had descended from heaven upon him,[138] and Elisha's ministry continued from there.

All of this is, in my view, the reason why Elijah must return. Elijah went up the same fiery ascent as the earlier translations. In the last days the system that began at first with Zion going up to heaven, will invert. It is going to open again, but this time instead of Zion leaving, Zion is going to stay and will be joined by those who went away, instead returning through the fiery ascent. Those who

---

[133] *Id.* v. 10.

[134] D&C 84:21-22.

[135] 2 Kings 2:11-12. Interestingly he cried out, as the event took place: "My father, my father!"

[136] *Id.* v. 13.

[137] *Id.* v. 14.

[138] Others knew this as well. See 2 Kings 2:15.

ascended will come again back through the corridor, to join a small group prepared to endure such glory. There is this marvelous description given to Enoch of when they return, they will fall on one another's necks and they will kiss one another.[139] Because Zion below and Zion above will be reunited.

The purpose of the return of Elijah, which Joseph talked about being a yet future event in Nauvoo, has everything to do with the return of Zion and the Lord's Second Coming. You can look at the *Teachings of the Prophet Joseph Smith* to find references to what I'm covering next. But that book is taken from the diaries of those who were present and recorded what they heard Joseph say. The diaries of the audience on the days Joseph gave the talks have been amalgamated into a single account which appears as the *Teachings*. These various accounts were compiled into a consolidated version and edited for grammar, punctuation and spelling, which is what you have in the *Teachings of the Prophet Joseph Smith*. But if you want the actual journals or diaries, that is found in the *Words of Joseph Smith*. Unfortunately that book is now out of print, and it is extravagantly expensive if you decide to buy a copy. The last I heard they were going for over $300, and, that copy was not in very good condition. However, you can find a copy through an LDS electronic library rather inexpensively. I understand there is work being done by Andy Ehat to bring it back into print, as well as to add a second volume to it which is to include comparable information taken from the Kirtland era talks of Joseph Smith. The *Words of Joseph Smith* in its current form is a compilation of only the Nauvoo era discourses. If the new project gets completed, it will be a two volume set covering both Nauvoo and Kirtland.

---

[139] Moses 7:63.

Well, to resume the topic, we go to January of 1844 in Nauvoo. This is some eight years post-Kirtland Temple appearance of Elijah.[140] On January 7, 1844, Joseph delivered a talk in front of Robert E. Foster's hotel, near the Nauvoo Temple. I am going to quote from Wilford Woodruff's Journal as the account of the talk that day. Joseph discussed the importance of Elijah, and said the following:

> "The Bible says, 'I will send you Elijah before the great and dreadful day of the Lord Come that he shall turn the hearts of the fathers to the children & the hearts of the Children to their fathers lest I Come & smite the whole earth with a Curse,' Now the word turn here should be translated (bind or seal) But what is the object of this important mission or how is it to be fulfilled, The keys are to be delivered the spirit of Elijah is to Come, [141]The gospel to be established the Saints of God gathered, Zion built up, & and the Saints to Come up as saviors on Mount Zion but how are they to become Saviors on mount Zion[?] by building temples erecting Baptismal fonts & going forth & receiving all the ordinances, Baptisms, Confirmations, washings, annoint-ings ordinations & sealing powers upon our heads in behalf of all our Progenitors who are dead & redeem them that they may Come forth in the first resurrection & be exalted to thrones of glory with us, &"[142]

What comes next is quite important, and I want to call attention to it before reading it. Joseph is about to lament the condition of

---

[140]   D&C 110 is dated April 3, 1836.

[141]   Notice Joseph's phrasing is future. The keys "are to be delivered" rather than they "had been delivered." The "spirit of Elijah is to come" and not that it had already come in 1836.

[142]   *Words of Joseph Smith*, 318, spelling and punctuation as in original, all footnotes omitted, from this and subsequent excerpts which follow.

the Saints then in Nauvoo. And it is quite important, I think, that this critical talk given by Joseph is recorded by no one in the audience other than Wilford Woodruff.[143] Thankfully Bro. Woodruff did so. But here is a statement of such terrible importance that it can change your entire understanding of what Joseph was teaching, and only a single person present bothers to record it. Well, Joseph laments:

> "I would to God that this temple was now done that we might go into it & go to work & improve our time & make use of the seals while they are on the earth & the Saints have none to much time to save & redeem their dead, & gather together their living relatives that they may be saved also, before the earth will be smitten & the Consumption decreed falls upon the world."[144]

Joseph lamented that the "seals" were still, with him "on the earth." But he noted that the Saints should be making use of them, in the Temple, "while they are [yet] on the earth." It implies, of course, that the available time was drawing to an end. That the haste required by the Lord[145] to have the Nauvoo Temple built was because a real threat existed that these seals were going to be lost to the Saints.[146] The consequence of failing to have these things accomplished while the seals were on the earth was that "the earth will be smitten[147] and the consumption decreed[148] would fall upon the

---

[143]   Willard Richards only notes the weather "was somewhat unpleasant." As to the talk, he recorded Joseph spoke "on sealing the hearts of the fathers to the children & the heart of the children to the fathers." *Id.,* 319.

[144]   *Id.,* 318.

[145]   D&C 124:26, 31.

[146]   *Id.* v. 32.

[147]   D&C 2:3.

[148]   D&C 87:6.

world." Joseph had made a hard bargain to get time in which to res-
cue some portion of the family of man from this looming
catastrophe.[149]

This is the talk, and this the place in the talk, when Joseph laments the Saints' failure to accept the truth. In the context of Elijah's mission, turning hearts to the fathers, and using the seals then
available on the earth, Joseph speaks of our hard heads, resistance
to truth, and flying to pieces when something new is taught about
the work of God. He continues:

> "Their has been a great difficulty in getting anything into
> the heads of this generation it has been like splitting hem-
> lock knots with a Corn doger for a wedge & a pumpkin for
> a beetle, Even the Saints are slow to understand I have tried
> for a number of years to get the minds of the Saints pre-
> pared to receive the things of God, but we frequently see
> some of them after suffering all they have for the work of
> God will fly to pieces like glass as soon as any thing Comes
> that is Contrary to their traditions, they Cannot stand the
> fire at all, How many will be able to abide a Celestial law &
> go through to receive their exhaltation I am unable to say
> but many are Called & few are Chosen."[150]

The Saints of that day were unwilling to hear from Joseph
about these doctrines. Therefore they left us with a single version of
his talk about this most important subject, given on January 7, 1844.
Joseph would be dead six months later. The catastrophe of his
death was, of course, unanticipated by them at the time. Therefore
their indifference may seem somewhat excusable. When, however,
the importance of the topic is weighed in the balance, how is anyone to conclude that either they, or we, are excused from careful,

---

[149]   D&C 124:1. I discuss this verse at length in *Passing the Heavenly Gift*.

[150]   *Words of Joseph Smith*, 319.

solemn and ponderous investigation into this topic? Even if considering it causes us to fear, we should trust that a loving Heavenly Father will not leave us in the dark about such matters. And, of course, the first step to repenting and reclaiming what God offers is always to awaken and arise from your pitiful condition lying in the dust. To repent, and return to Him will always allow us to regain His grace. But unless we awaken, we are not in a position to even attempt to repent. We don't know we need to! We remain in our slumber, lying in the dust, unredeemed, unawake, and without understanding which might have saved some few of us.

Joseph revisited the topic of Elijah's meaning again in a talk given on March 10, 1844. When he picks up the subject again to discuss Elijah, he says, "The spirit power & calling of Elijah is that ye have power to hold the keys of the revelations ordinances, oricles powers & endowments of the fulness of the Melchezedek Priesthood & of the Kingdom of God on the Earth & to receive, obtain and perform all the ordinances belonging to the Kingdom of God even unto the sealing of the hearts of the fathers unto the children & the hearts of the **children unto the fathers even those who are in heaven.**"[151]

Notice the connection between these parties. It is not to connect you to your kindred dead. They are in the world of spirits. They are not "in heaven." Joseph is talking about a connection of your hearts to "the hearts of the fathers who are in heaven." That is the mission of Elijah. If you will receive it, this is the spirit of Elijah: That we redeem our dead, but then connect ourselves with our "fathers which are in heaven." Our dead are saved through us, but we are saved by connecting to our "fathers in heaven." Who are our "fathers in heaven" to whom we must be connected? If all we do is

---

[151]   *Id.* 329, emphasis added.

connect ourselves to our dead, then neither they nor we are connected to the "fathers in heaven." So it becomes quite important to
understand why Joseph is talking in these strange terms. Who are
these "fathers in heaven" to whom we must form a connection? We
want the power of Elijah to seal those who dwell on earth to those
which dwell "in heaven." Merely connecting the earthly to their kindred dead will not suffice. Joseph is explaining something more
cosmic in this integration of generations. It is greater than mere
genealogy.

Remember, those who are in the spirit world, our dead, are in
need of redemption. They don't have these ordinances yet. We are
supposed to take care of that for them. Our dead are the ones that
need redemption from us, and cannot be the "fathers in heaven"
Joseph is discussing. They cannot be "in heaven," because they need
us to be redeemed. We need to be redeemed by our connecting to
"the fathers who are in heaven."

This is important enough for Joseph to have focused on it in
the remaining months of his life. As we have seen, Joseph expressed
exasperation at the hard heads of the Saints, who would not listen
to new information. Let us not repeat the error. We must do something more to avoid being "utterly wasted" at the Lord's return.[152]
We must connect ourselves to "the fathers in heaven." Joseph understood this doctrine.

Unlike most Latter-day Saints, it is my view that the idea you go
to the temple and do genealogical work to respond to the coming of
Elijah does not, indeed cannot, conform to the description here
from Joseph Smith. Our ancestors, our kindred dead, need to be
redeemed. They all have an interest in you and your life. The work

---

[152]   D&C 2:3.

that is being done on behalf of the dead, needs to be done. But the gulf which must be bridged through the work of Elijah, in the words of Joseph Smith "to form a bond or connection," is not completed unless we have been sealed to "the fathers in heaven." Those there include, of course, as we have seen, Enoch's City and Melchizedek's City, and extend further to Abraham, Isaac and Jacob.[153]

Well, we should ask ourselves about Elijah's role in all this. If the "fathers in heaven" are going to return, then what must be done to prepare for them? If they will bring with them—or perhaps it might be more correct to invert that—if it is the Lord who will bring them, what must be done to live in His presence?[154] How does a person qualify to survive such an appearance?[155] What kind of priestly authority allows a man to behold God's face and live? These questions all have answers in the scriptures. They are not hidden from us. Joseph's revelations are as consistent as Joseph's sermons in giving us what we need to know to preserve ourselves for the day of the Lord's return.

All of this does involve Elijah. He is not, as we often tell ourselves, the last person to hold the sealing power. That would have been Peter.[156] Or, since we don't have accurate dates for their respective deaths, it may have been Nephi,[157] on this continent. But you can know for a certainty that it was *NOT* Elijah. Therefore anyone who teaches Elijah's return is connected only to sealing power

---

153   See D&C 132:37.

154   Consider what happens when someone enters His presence who is not prepared: Mormon 9:2-6.

155   See D&C 84:21-22.

156   Matt. 16:18, though it was likely John—a matter beyond this discussion.

157   Helaman 10:7.

used to connect ourselves to our kindred dead, but which does not also include connecting us with the "fathers in heaven," does not understand the truth as yet. Joseph's description of Elijah's mission included a connection using Elijah's seals between the living and the "fathers in heaven." The kindred dead are beneficiaries of that also; but the link, the thing which would prevent mankind from being "utterly wasted" at the Lord's return,[158] was this connection to the "fathers in heaven." He proclaimed it to an indifferent audience at Nauvoo, who hardly took note of the teaching. Today, as descendants from the Nauvoo audience, we use still Joseph's vocabulary. We talk about "seals" and about "sealing." But we have a vastly different picture in mind than the one Joseph was setting out. We know nothing about the connection to the "fathers in heaven" and instead focus on the genealogical connection to our kindred dead. No matter how much we connect them to us, we cannot help them, nor can we be helped either, if we do not have ourselves bound to "the fathers in heaven." We will all be "utterly wasted" unless we reform the correct connection and use the correct authority to accomplish it.

Here, then, we have finally arrived at Elijah's significance as the one who must first return. He was not the last one living who held the sealing power, though he did in fact possess it. Instead, he is vital as the last one to make the ascent from earth to heaven.[159] He rose up through the fiery corridor, and went to God's presence. He joined the "fathers in heaven" who are to return. He last opened the way by his physical ascent. He will be the first to physically descend through the fiery corridor to return from heaven to dwell again on

---

[158]   D&C 2:3.

[159]   John the Beloved's ascent and subsequent ministry connect him to this end of the corridor. John's ministry here includes responsibility to prepare mortal man to come up to Zion. See D&C 7:6.

earth. His return will not be made in a temporary opening.[160] We've had plenty of those.[161] His return will open a permanent, fixed stairway between the "fathers in heaven" and those who are prepared for the return of Zion. Zion will be overshadowed by the Lord's glory.[162] The fiery corridor, or pillar of fire,[163] or ladder to heaven,[164] or conduit into heaven,[165] or chariot of fire,[166] will be opened by Elijah's descent. It will remain over Zion and will be visible there.[167] It will not be temporary. It will be the place from which the first preparations for the Second Coming begin. At that location a small group will be prepared to endure this opening. They, and those called to join with them, will escape being "utterly wasted" at the unveiling of our Lord in glory at His return. It is Elijah who will restore the hearts of the fathers to the children or, in other words, he will reestablish the lost corridor between heaven and earth that connects those in heaven with those on earth.[168]

This fiery path needs to be opened beforehand. The path, once it opens, will allow men on the earth to be prepared for the coming

---

[160] The temporary opening on 3 April 1836 in the Kirtland Temple, therefore, could not fulfill the entire mission. This is why Joseph continued to speak of Elijah's future return even after the Kirtland Temple event.

[161] Joseph had a temporary opening in the First Vision (JS-H 1:16), and again when Moroni appeared (Id. v. 30). Likewise, the Nephites had it open in the presence of 2,500 believers (3 Ne. 17:24). There have been others, also, for whom the fiery ascent has opened, but they have all been temporary.

[162] See, e.g., D&C 64:41; 133:32; 136:31; 84:32, among other places.

[163] See Exo. 13:22.

[164] Gen. 28:12.

[165] See JS-H 1:43.

[166] See 2 Kings 2:11.

[167] 2 Ne. 14:5.

[168] See D&C 128:17.

again of those who are Zion above. Well, Elijah answers to this. Joseph continued in this March 10th discussion teaching:

> "in the days of Noah God destroyed the world by a flood
> & has promised to destroy it by fire in the last days but be-
> fore it took place Elijah should first come & turn the hearts
> of the Fathers to the Children &c now comes the point
> what is this office & work of Elijah, it is one of the greatest
> & most important subjects that God has revealed, He
> should send Elijah to seal the children to the fathers & fa-
> thers to the Children… I wish you to understand this sub-
> ject for it is important & if you will receive it this is the
> spirit of Elijah that we redeem our dead & **connect our-
> selves with our fathers which are in heaven** & seal up
> our dead to come forth in the first resurrection & here we
> want the power of Elijah to seal those who dwell on earth
> to those which dwell in heaven."[169]

This quote divides mankind into three groups: First, us, the living, are required to do work using Elijah's guidance. Second, the "fathers which are in heaven" to whom we must have a bond to avoid being wasted at the Lord's return.[170] Third, "our dead" who are intended to benefit from our connection and qualify to be resurrected into a saved line of priestly authorities stretching through us to the "fathers which are in heaven." We must be sealed to "the fathers which are in heaven" in order to be saved. "Our dead" must be redeemed and sealed to us, that they may also inherit eternal life with us. Doing a sealing between our dead and ourselves, however, is not enough and only connects two of the three groups together. Until we are also connected to the third group, that is "our fathers which are in heaven," we remain vulnerable to being "utterly wasted

---

169 *Words of Joseph Smith*, 329, emphasis added.

170 Some of those visited with Joseph in the Kirtland Temple when Elijah made a preliminary appearance. That foreshadows a greater, yet future, return.

at His coming." Joseph knew what he was talking about. He used the correct terms and outlined the correct path. We have just ignored it.

Joseph continued:

"Again, the doctrin or sealing power of Elijah is as follows if you have power to seal on earth & in heaven then we should be Crafty, the first thing you do you go & seal on earth your sons and daughters unto yourself, & yourself **unto your fathers in eternal glory,**"[171]

Notice that. You seal "yourself unto your fathers in eternal glory!" These are not your kindred dead, who have died without the Gospel are in the Spirit World, awaiting salvation from your efforts on their behalf. They do not live "in eternal glory" because their hopes are dependent upon you performing the required connections between them, you and "the fathers who dwell in glory." This connection is to come, if it comes to us, from Elijah's return.

Who are "the fathers who dwell in glory?" Well, go back to the revelation in which Joseph Smith received the sealing power, D&C 132:49. There you learn the sealing power was conferred upon Joseph by God's voice: "I the Lord thy God will be with thee even unto the end of the world and through all eternity for verily I seal upon your exaltation. Prepare your throne for you **in the kingdom of my Father, with Abraham your father**" (emphasis added.) This is Joseph's calling and election. Then, in verse 46 Joseph is given the power to seal: "I say unto you whatsoever you seal on earth shall be sealed in heaven. Whatsoever ye shall bind on earth in my name by my word, saith the Lord, it shall be eternally bound in the heavens. Whosoever's sins are remitted on earth shall be eternally remitted

---

[171] *Id.*, 331.

eternally in heaven" and so on. This reference to Christ's "Father, and [Joseph's] father Abraham" is important. The connection was made between Joseph and Abraham, one of the "fathers who dwell in glory" because as soon as Joseph received the sealing authority and was promised exaltation, the Lord immediately describes the effect of the Lord sealing Joseph to eternal life and exaltation. It connected Joseph with "the fathers who dwell in glory." It made Joseph a living member of the family of the exalted.

Just before this in verse 37, the revelation also clarifies the status of Abraham, Isaac and Jacob. Those three are among the "fathers who dwell in glory" in the heavens. As the revelation puts it: "Because they did none other things in that which they were commanded they have entered into their exaltation according to the promises and **sit upon thrones and are not angels but are Gods.**"[172] (Emphasis added.) This is Abraham, Isaac, and Jacob. These are the ones who are now Gods. The "seals" which Joseph tells us we should be "crafty" and use for our salvation, are what could connect us to the "fathers" Abraham, Isaac and Jacob, who dwell in glory. They are part of the Family of God. They are among those who are exalted.

I think that Christ was deliberate about everything He said during His ministry, including the analogies He used in the stories He told. When Christ took occasion in the Parable of Lazarus and the Rich Man, to tell us about the status of individuals in heaven, we should take careful note. When the beggar Lazarus died, he was "carried by the angels into Abraham's bosom."[173] Lazarus leaves this world accompanied by angels, and is taken to Abraham's bosom.

---

[172] These fathers are already exalted. For them it is not future. They occupy a throne now.

[173] Luke 16:22.

The definition of reward in the afterlife is to go to "the bosom of Abraham."

The rich man dies and is in torment. But Jesus does not tell us the rich man cried out to God for relief, instead Christ has the tormented man cry out to Abraham.[174] That is important, as well, but a detour from what we're discussing, so it must be left at that.

When Jesus is describing positions of authority in the afterlife, He uses Abraham as the key to relief from torment. The deceased looks to Abraham's position and knows there is relief there. The man petitions: "Father Abraham, have mercy on me, and send Lazarus, that he may dip the tip of his finger in water, and cool my tongue; for I am tormented in this flame."[175] Ask yourself if being connected to "the fathers which dwell in heaven" or, in other words Abraham (among others) is any clearer a topic from the roles Christ uses to teach us in this parable.

It continues: "But Abraham said, Son, remember that thou in thy lifetime received the good things, and likewise Lazarus evil things: but now he is comforted, and thou are tormented."[176] There is an equation. Everything will balance. You rich people had good before, but allowed Lazarus to suffer from evil you could have relieved. Now it is put back into balance. In the immediate afterlife you get to suffer, so you may understand the error of your way. You may at last understand how charity is critical to make the universe whole. See, if you are one who chooses to inflict tears (or even ignore tears you might have wiped away), then that will be recompensed to you. And if you wipe away tears, from others, that will be

---

174   *Id.* v. 24.

175   *Id.*

176   *Id.* v. 25.

returned to you as well. Because what will be restored unto you is exactly, as we began with Alma, what you send out.[177] It is an equation after all.

The rich man cried out, "I pray thee therefore, father, that thou wouldest send him to my father's house: For I have five brethren; that he may testify to them, lest they also come into this place of torment. Abraham said unto him, They have Moses and the prophets; let them hear them. And he said, Nay, father Abraham; but if one went into them from the dead, they will repent. He said unto him, If they hear not Moses and the prophets, neither will they be persuaded, though one rose from the dead."[178] I've discussed this parable more fully in *Come, Let Us Adore Him*, and would refer you to that discussion. Here we are only concerned with the high status in which Jesus puts Abraham in the afterlife. He used this parable in exactly the same way as Section 132 refers to Abraham; that is, as if he becomes godlike in the afterlife, an arbiter of men's fate.

One of the things we have mistaken in our Elijah theology also is the incorrect notion that on the Mount of Transfiguration Elijah and Moses appeared to Peter, James and John. We analogize it to the Kirtland Temple appearance described in Section 110. We also connect that to sealing power in both dispensations.[179] However, Joseph Smith did not teach that and therefore we ought to re-look at the topic so we have Elijah's role as clearly set out as we can get it.

On the Mount of Transfiguration, Elijah did not appear. It was John the Baptist. At least if Joseph Smith understood the matter

---

[177]   Alma 41:15.

[178]   Luke 16:27-31.

[179]   Christ gave Peter the sealing power in Matt. 16:19. Some six days later the events on the Mount of Transfiguration occurred. (Matt. 17:1-9.)

correctly, it was John the Baptist. First, we need the account from Matthew 17, which reads:

> 1 And after six days Jesus taketh Peter, James, and John his brother, and bringeth them up into an high mountain apart,

> 2 And was transfigured before them: and his face did shine as the sun, and his raiment was white as the light.

> 3 And, behold, there appeared unto them Moses and Elias talking with him.

> 4 Then answered Peter, and said unto Jesus, Lord, it is good for us to be here: if thou wilt, let us make here three tabernacles; one for thee, and one for Moses, and one for Elias.

> 5 While he yet spake, behold, a bright cloud overshadowed them: and behold a voice out of the cloud, which said, This is my beloved Son, in whom I am well pleased; hear ye him.

> 6 And when the disciples heard it, they fell on their face, and were sore afraid.

> 7 And Jesus came and touched them, and said, Arise, and be not afraid.

> 8 And when they had lifted up their eyes, they saw no man, save Jesus only.

> 9 And as they came down from the mountain, Jesus charged them, saying, Tell the vision to no man, until the Son of man be risen again from the dead.

> 10 And his disciples asked him, saying, Why then say the scribes that Elias must first come?

> 11 And Jesus answered and said unto them, Elias truly shall first come, and restore all things.

12 But I say unto you, That Elias is come already, and they knew him not, but have done unto him whatsoever they listed. Likewise shall also the Son of man suffer of them.

13 Then the disciples understood that he spake unto them of John the Baptist.

Therefore on the Mount of Transfiguration the "Elias" mentioned is John the Baptist, not Elijah. When Joseph Smith rendered a correct translation for the event in Mark, he makes it even more clear. Beginning at Mark 9:2 and going through verse 4 we read:

2 And after six days Jesus taketh with him Peter, and James, and John, and leadeth them up into an high mountain apart by themselves: and he was transfigured before them.

3 And his raiment became shining, exceeding white as snow; so as no fuller on earth can white them.

4 And there appeared unto them Elias with Moses, *or, in other words, John the Baptist and Moses*: and they were talking with Jesus.

In the Joseph Smith translation he inserts into verse 4 "or in other words, John the Baptist and Moses." Therefore, Joseph rewrote the verse to clarify the identify of who was on the Mount at the time of transfiguration. It was not Elijah. It was John the Baptist. If Joseph Smith understood the matter [and I think he did], then it was John the Baptist and Moses who appeared on the Mount of Transfiguration. We, however, have instead adopted a long tradition of associating the appearance there with Elijah and Moses, which is part of our Elijah theology.[180] If this is important enough that we will be "utterly wasted" if we get it wrong, then it probably deserves the kind of careful consideration recommended earlier in this paper. But, again, I want to remind you that I am offering my view, and explaining why I hold the view I do. You can disagree and accept what is traditionally taught among the Saints; if you do you will be in a very large company. My view is held by only a few. So if you believe there is safety through numbers, you will not find that safety thinking as I do. I'm rather a lone voice crying from outside, and not in the well-established broad, mainstream thinking of the Latter-day Saints. This is, of course, something church authorities have warned you against.[181] I want to emphasize, therefore, that I'm only explaining my views and why I hold them. They are intended only to stimulate thought, nothing more.

When I consider this matter, I reach a different conclusion than the generally accepted Elijah narrative. I think when it comes to Elijah's role and mission, his purpose will be fulfilled on the cusp of the Lord's return, in order to open the fiery ascent through which the Zion above can return. That ministry was still future in March, 1844 and it is still future today. If it was still future some three

---

[180] The most recent restatement of our tradition can be found in last General Conference (October 2011) in the talk titled: *The Hearts of the Children Shall Turn*. In it we were taught, among other things: "Elijah appeared with Moses on the Mount of Transfiguration (see Matthew 17:3) and conferred this authority upon Peter, James, and John. Elijah appeared again with Moses and others on April 3, 1836, in the Kirtland Temple and conferred the same keys upon Joseph Smith and Oliver Cowdery."

[181] For example, Elder Bruce R. McConkie gave a talk on January 10, 1982 in which he taught: "Now is the time and the day of your salvation, so if you're working zealously in this life – though you haven't fully overcome the world and you haven't done all you hoped you might do—you're still going to be saved. You don't have to do what Jacob said, 'Go beyond the mark.' You don't have to live a life that's truer than true. You don't have to have an excessive zeal that becomes fanatical and becomes unbalancing. What you have to do is stay in the mainstream of the Church and live as upright and decent people live in the Church – keeping the commandments, paying your tithing, serving in the organizations of the Church, loving the Lord, staying on the straight and narrow path." (*The Probationary Test of Mortality*, delivered at the University of Utah.)

months before Joseph's death, then it was not satisfied by the Kirtland Temple events. Elijah's purpose is to make it possible to reunite
those that dwell above in glory with those that dwell below on the
earth. Those who dwell below for whom Elijah's mission will be
relevant will need to be capable of bearing the presence of the
Lord. They must be able to come back into His presence and endure the glory of it all rather than being consumed by it.[182] For this,
of course, there are some requirements.[183] But these will be those
who will dwell in peace in Zion, where He will come and dwell
among a City of Peace, having all things in common, and possessing
one heart.

Another relevant topic is "the promises made to the fathers."
What were those? We try to focus on the children, since we regard
ourselves as that. But it is equally important to know what the
promises were to the fathers, and who they were. Once you have the
right fathers and the right promises in mind, it leads you to understand more clearly Elijah's role in fulfilling the promises.

Abraham is, as we saw, the "father of the righteous." All those
who live after his day will need to be connected to him if they are to
be saved. Salvation is, after all, a family affair. God's family will be
composed of Abraham's line, including any living after his day who
receive the Gospel. In the promises made to Abraham, the Lord
covenanted that "as many as receive this Gospel shall be called after
thy name, and shall be accounted thy seed, and shall rise up and
bless thee, as their father[.]" (Abr. 2:10.) These are important matters. When anyone "receives this Gospel"—meaning the same Gos-

---

[182]   See D&C 84:20-22.

[183]   See Abraham 2:8-11. Abraham was, as we have seen, such a person. He entered the
Lord's presence. The Lord told Abraham about his "seed" or, in other words, those who
would similarly come to know God and receive the same standing as did Abraham.

pel which Abraham received—then they will acknowledge Abraham as their father. But the covenant goes further. "And I will bless them that bless thee, and curse them that curse thee; and in thee (that is, in thy Priesthood) and in thy seed (that is, thy Priesthood), ... shall all the families of the earth be blessed." (*Id.* v. 11.) There is a connection between Priesthood, Abraham, salvation and being the "seed" of father Abraham. Priesthood is a connection between those in heaven and those on earth. Unless there is a connection between a man and his fathers or brethren in heaven, there is no power in his priesthood.[184] This is the reason why Moroni explained Elijah's return was connected to priesthood.[185] Malachi does not make this connection in his prophecy.[186] Nor does Christ point out the priesthood connection to Elijah.[187] All of the accounts, however, connect Elijah's return to connecting the "children" – who are to inherit Abraham's Priesthood as his "seed" – and "the fathers." Moroni merely clarified this connection would give power to the priesthood, because once connected to "the fathers who dwell in heaven" the children are in possession of priesthood. They are part of the Heavenly Family, which is a Priesthood order.

As I explained in *Passing the Heavenly Gift,* Joseph was working to re-establish this connection in the Nauvoo Temple. He received a revelation promising the "fullness" which the Saints had

---

[184] See D&C 121:36.

[185] See D&C 2:1: "Behold, I will reveal unto you the priesthood, by the hand of Elijah..."

[186] Mal. 4:5: "Behold, I will send you Elijah the prophet before the coming of the great and dreadful day of the Lord;"

[187] Christ had the Nephites add the prophecy to their scriptures. When He does, however, He repeats the formula of Malachi: "Behold, I will send you Elijah the prophet before the coming of the great and dreadful day of the Lord." (3 Ne. 25:5.)

lost, would be restored again, if the Temple were completed.[188] The fullness would come because the Lord would visit with His people there.[189] If the Lord visited with His people, it would have been Zion. But the Lord did not come to Nauvoo, and that Temple was utterly destroyed, not one stone left atop the other.

Joseph wanted the Saints to enter into the Lord's presence. He began installing the Temple rites, including beginning the endowment above his red brick store. The endowment instructs the initiated in the path back to the presence of God. However, he died before the Saints completed the required Temple for the Lord to come and restore the fullness. It is clear, however, that Joseph anticipated there would eventually be more added to the Temple. In fact, he connected Elijah's mission not just to sealing, but also to

---

[188] D&C 124:28.

[189] *Id.*

everything including animal sacrifice.[190] While this is a little-studied topic, this was mentioned early in the Restoration by John the Baptist.[191] That rite does not presently exist among the Saints, and the idea of "the sons of Levi offering an offering" is not connected to animal sacrifice in the minds of the Saints.[192] Joseph Smith foretold this but did not live to accomplish it. We now have the responsibility to preserve,[193] and act, on those ordinances he was able to

---

[190]   "Why send Elijah because he holds the Keys of the Authority to administer in all the ordinances of the priesthood and without the authority is given the ordinances could not be administered in righteousness. It is a very prevalent opinion that the sacrifices which were offered were entirely consumed, this was not the case if you read Leviticus [2] Chap [2-3] verses you will observe that the priests took a part as a memorial and offered it up before the Lord, while the remainder was kept for the benefit maintenance of the priests. So that the offerings and sacrifices are not all consumed upon the Alter, but the blood is sprinkled and the fat and certain other portions are consumed These sacrifices as well as every ordinance belonging to the priesthood will when the temple of the Lord shall be built and the Sons Levi be purified be fully restored and attended to then all their powers, ramifications, and blessings—this the Sons of Levi shall be purified. ever was and will exist when the powers of the Melchizedek Priesthood are sufficiently manifest. Else how can the restitution of all things spoken of by all the Holy Prophets be brought to pass. It is not to be understood that, the law of Moses will be established again with all it rights and variety of ceremonies, this had never been spoken off by the prophets but those things which existed prior Moses's day *viz* Sacrifice will be continued—It may be asked by some what necessity for Sacrifice since the great Sacrifice was offered? In answer to which if Repentance Baptism and faith were necessary to Salvation existed prior to the days of Christ what necessity for them since that time" [This is taken from the only discourse of Joseph Smith which was written before being delivered. It was given October 5, 1840. The original is in the hand writing of Robert B. Thompson (a clerk for Joseph Smith); maintained in the LDS Church Archives. It is cited in Smith, William V. A, *Joseph Smith Commentary on the Book of Abraham: An Introduction to the Study of the Book of Abraham.* 2nd ed. Provo, UT: The Book of Abraham Project, 2002, 65-66.]

[191]   See JS-H 1:69 and Oliver Cowdery's version in the footnote at the end of the JS-H.

[192]   All those ordained in the church are reminded of the "oath and covenant of the Priesthood" found at D&C 84:33-39. This oath makes all who hold the church's two priesthoods responsible for becoming "sons of Aaron" and "sons of Moses"—both of whom are of Levi.

[193]   It is a terrible offense to God to change His ordinances. See Isaiah 24:5. Joseph also instructed that "Ordinances instituted in the heavens before the foundation of the world, in the priesthood, for the salvation of men, are not to be altered or changed...He set the temple ordinances to be the same forever and ever and set Adam to watch over them, to reveal them from heaven to man, or to send angels to reveal them." (*DHC* 4:208.)

restore. They can bring us back to the Lord's presence. The Lord, of course, can and will instruct us further. That was the anticipation for the Nauvoo Temple, for the Lord was going to be the one who restored the fullness there. As I discuss in *Passing the Heavenly Gift*, it did not occur at the time. It remains a future event, connected to establishing Zion, still.

I would suggest the peace of Zion is different than some people believe, also. I do not think Zion's peace is related to taking up arms and fighting. It is true, of course, that Zion will not take up arms against others.[194] But that is secondary. What is primary is the basis for that peace. It comes having shed your sins and being able to endure the presence of the Lord. Because these are those people who have "let virtue garnish their thoughts unceasingly because their bowels have been full of charity towards all men, and to the household of faith."[195] Can you imagine that? Can you imagine that it is necessary that you have charity for those who are within your own household of faith! Can you imagine that each of us need to tolerate, and even love, those inside our own community of belief who think you are an emissary of the devil? Who "have a testimony" and do not want to hear anything new or different from their proudly held errors? Who think you are an apostate if you search more deeply into the faith than they will ever do? Toward them we must all show charity? Well, yes, of course. They get to abuse and despitefully use you.[196] And you must, as Christ both taught[197] and lived,[198] must return good for evil. That is His stan-

---

[194] D&C 45:69.

[195] D&C 121:45.

[196] Matt. 5:43-45.

[197] Matt. 5:44.

[198] Luke 23:34.

dard, and He expects anyone who will come up to live with Him in Zion to live the standard. Otherwise they cannot dwell with Him.

We must also "let virtue garnish thy thoughts unceasingly." Because, you see, if you are not so constituted within your own heart—where there can't be any lies—if within your heart you are not at peace through charity toward those who would, in the name of your own religion despitefully use you, then your "confidence [cannot] wax strong in the presence of God."[199] And all of this is necessarily connected to "the doctrine of the priesthood."[200] This is because you can never know the Master whom you have not served.[201] The service which brings you to Him, which lets you understand Him, and which gives you insight into the "doctrine of His Priesthood" comes only by taking up your cross and following Him.[202] Not as a proud hypocrite claiming you have the truth and are better than others, but as the servant of others[203] bearing their scorn and patiently testifying to the truth they do not want to hear. As the letter Joseph wrote from Liberty Jail states: "Let thy bowels also be full of charity towards all men and to the household of faith, and let virtue garnish thy thoughts unceasingly, then shall thy confidence wax strong in the presence of God; and the doctrine of the priesthood shall distill upon thy soul as the dews of heaven."[204] Doctrine and truth will just condense upon your soul because when

---

[199]   D&C 121:45.

[200]   Id.

[201]   Mosiah 5:13.

[202]   Mark 8:39.

[203]   Matt. 23:11.

[204]   D&C 121:45.

you do that, you reach 'dew point.' You come to a place in which it is possible for God's mercy to water your soul.[205]

The letter continues: "The Holy Ghost shall be thy constant companion, and they scepter an unchanging scepter of righteousness and truth;" [I need to pause there for a moment because there are so many who cry out: "I want a scepter! Because can't you use those things to bash people in the head and say 'big me, little you?'" Scepters have nothing to do with ruling and reigning. Scepters have to do with serving and kneeling. He who made Himself the least, even though He was the greatest, kneeled and washed the dirt from the feet of those who in every respect He excelled. He wanted to give *them* the chief seats. He didn't envy those He raised. He didn't envy those that presided over Him.[206] He declared the truth and He declared it boldly because He knew what the truth was. To the extent that He could do so diplomatically, He did. When the moment came and it was necessary to lay it out, it was He who chose the moment of sacrifice. It was He that went up to Jerusalem to be crucified, and it was He who in righteous fury cleansed the Temple. He provoked the reaction that resulted in His own sacrifice at the appropriate moment, because the fullness of time had come for that offering on that Passover. I talk about that in a chapter in *Come Let Us Adore Him* and won't repeat it here.

Well, to return from the interruption: "The Holy Ghost shall be thy constant companion, and they scepter an unchanging scepter of righteousness and truth; and thy dominion shall be an everlasting dominion, and without compulsory means it shall flow unto thee forever and ever."[207] You cannot compel these things. You can qual-

---

[205] See John 4:10.

[206] Matt. 23:2-3.

[207] D&C 121:46.

ify by submitting to the conditions. But when you submit to His will it flows to you naturally, and without compulsion. This form of "dominion" is dominion over your own soul. You conquer your desires, appetites and passions, and you confine them entirely to the bounds which the Lord has prescribed. This begins in your own thoughts, when you let virtue garnish them unceasingly. Question your own motives, not others'. Question your own obedience and service, not others. Be quick to judge yourself, and cover the mistakes of others with charity.[208] Pray for your critics and those who you know offend God by the things they are doing. They are ignorant, and if you do not ask for God's mercy on their behalf they will never know enough to ask for it themselves. Make intercession for them. (If you've not read about that in *The Second Comforter: Conversing With the Lord Through the Veil*, then I would refer you to that discussion there.)

The peace in Zion is the same peace Joseph described in his letter from Liberty Jail, from which I have just been reading (D&C 121). That peace begins inside you. It is not merely the discipline of warfare and enforcement of rights through conflict. That will be the wicked's way to seek peace. For Zion, the peace comes from within.

Going back to the account of Enoch, we read about these issues there, as well. Concerning the priesthood, we read in Moses 6:7: "Now this same Priesthood, which was in the beginning, shall be in the end of the world also." Elijah's role is a priestly role. But the original Holy Order, the Holy Order after the Son of God, when there was a single form of Priesthood, which is to return at

---

[208] Joseph Smith taught: "If you do not accuse each other, God will not accuse you. If you have no accuser you will enter heaven, and if you will follow the revelations and instructions which God gives you through me, I will take you into heaven as my back load. If you will not accuse me, I will not accuse you. If you will throw a cloak of charity over my sins, I will over yours—for charity covereth a multitude of sins." *(DHC, 4:445.)*

the end. It includes "a fullness" because it has not be fractured apart by men qualifying for only piecemeal authority. But that is a vast topic and takes us afield from this subject. We hardly comprehend the nature of that order, which involves "the fathers" from Adam to Melchizedek, then restored again through Abraham and descended through him for five unbroken generations. The fullness of that story is not yet available in scripture for our study. We need to remain on Elijah's importance.

Well, when you add the promise that the same priesthood will return together with Christ's comment "as it was in the days of Noah, so shall also the coming of the Son of man be," you have something noteworthy. The "days of Noah" overlapped the time in which it was yet possible to be caught up to Enoch's Zion.[209] As we saw earlier, Enoch's City survived the flood of Noah by fleeing. This time, however, because of Elijah's coming ministry, there will be those who escape the upcoming fiery ordeal by connecting with heaven in advance. They will not be "wasted at His coming" because they are able to endure His presence.

Remember, the first Zion had seven High Priests with their posterity, who were righteous.[210] That posterity which were righteous were the families raised by these High Priests. I have to assume that included multiple generations. Even so, the original Zion to which the Lord came was essentially seven extended families. So it was quite small. This small group came at a time when the population of the earth may have reached in the billions, according to some estimates.

---

[209]   Moses 7:27.

[210]   D&C 107:53.

The Zion established by Enoch thereafter we don't have any geographic description or numeric description, apart from a single statement in the book of Jude. That statement is really quoting from an earlier text of Enoch. Jude refers to the return of Enoch "with ten-thousands of his saints."[211] Those kinds of numbers are not particularly reliable, because given the way in which numbers were symbols in those days, the error, if there is one, is an over-statement, not an understatement. In other words there would *not* be millions described as ten thousands; but there could be hundreds described as ten thousands. So it is again possible that Enoch's City may be less than the great numbers some have thought. It may be they number in the mere thousands, and not as many as 100,000. We don't know. But we shouldn't assume the numbers were necessarily great.

When it comes to Melchizedek's City of Peace, the area occupied was apparently an agrarian setting that could have been located on something that is as small as 20 city blocks of our current type. I doubt it would have numbered more than 1,000. Again, however, we do not know. But we shouldn't assume the numbers were significant; probably a branch or branches of a single family.

Whatever the numbers were, the significance of Zion is not, and never was, its numerosity. The significance of Zion is its spiritual endowment. It is the power of heaven, and not the voting block. It is not their big numbers which intimidate the ungodly. Even a handful is sufficient. Righteousness is a power in itself.

Remember from the account of John when they came to arrest the Savior. He asked who they were seeking. They said "Jesus of Nazareth." He declared, "I am He." The guard stood face to face

---

[211] Jude 1:14.

with righteousness. The imposing figure of the righteous Lord was enough to intimidate those who came with swords and with shields, protected and armed, while He was clothed only with the garments He had on and the force of righteousness within him. The guards "went backward, and fell to the ground."[212] At that moment in that garden, in that presence, confined to the person of one individual, there was Zion. I do not think the picture we have in our head of the role, mission, ministry and purpose of the return of Elijah in necessarily one that is accurate. Nor do I think that the role, mission and ministry and the effort of Elijah is something from our past. Just as Joseph predicted the future return in January and March of 1844, I think the role and mission of Elijah is intimately connected with the immediate return of Christ. He will open the capacity for a group of people, however few, who will be able to endure the burning accompanying Christ's return.[213] The heavens will be rolled together, like s scroll.[214] The Lord's glory will shine forth, untempered by the veil now in place.[215] The few who can endure this prevent the earth from being "utterly wasted at His coming."[216] Because they have already been prepared by Elijah, and others, for this great day, they will be able to greet the returning hosts of heaven, and fall upon one another's necks and kiss one another.[217]

Those few who are prepared will live in peace with one another. There will be, among them, no rivalry, no disparity, no hierarchy, and all things in common. These things are rather difficult when you

---

[212]   See John 18:4-6.

[213]   Malachi 4:1.

[214]   Isa. 34, 4; Rev. 6:14; D&C 88:95.

[215]   D&C 5:19.

[216]   D&C 2:3.

[217]   Moses 7:63.

have a society with "big" and "little" people; when you have important and wealthy in one portion of the society, and obscure and
poor in another group. We cannot be there because we have those
who are mighty and wonderful at the top, and those who are subservient and nothing at the bottom. Our society is sick, from top to
bottom.[218] We are not Zion, nor anything like it. Therefore the mission of Elijah will be as critical for us as it is for any other person
living today. Our church affiliation is of little benefit, until we awake
and arise to the point where we can stand in the Lord's presence.[219]

High Nibley used to talk, I think rather tongue in cheek, about
how he would be content to be nothing more than the door keeper
in the House of the Lord; because if he were he would be standing
next to "the keeper of the gate who is the Holy One of Israel who
employeth no servant there." (2 Ne. 9:41.) That idea is an important
one. The real House of the Lord is not a building. It is you.[220] If
you will permit Him, He will come to dwell there, and even bring
His Father to you.[221]

---

[218] See Isaiah 1:2-8: "Hear, O heavens, and give ear, O earth: for the Lord hath spoken,
I have nourished and brought up children, and they have rebelled against me. The ox
knoweth his owner, and the ass his master's crib: but Israel doth not know, my people
doth not consider. Ah sinful nation, a people laden with iniquity, a seed of evildoers,
children that are corrupters: they have forsaken the Lord, they have provoked the Holy
One of Israel unto anger, they are gone away backward. Why should ye be stricken any
more? Ye will revolt more and more: the whole head is sick, and the whole heart faint.
From the sole of the foot even unto the head there is no soundness in it; but wounds,
and bruises, and putrifying sores: they have not been closed, neither bound up, neither
mollified with ointment. Your country is desolate, your cities are burned with fire: your
land, strangers devour it in your presence, and it is desolate, as overthrown by strangers.
And the daughter of Zion is left as a cottage in a vineyard, as a lodge in a garden of
cucumbers, as a besieged city."

[219] See D&C 93:1.

[220] 1 Cor. 3:16-17.

[221] John 14:23.

Well, I wrote a book and I made some people angry, but I also returned some people back to the faith through that same book. And I don't want there to be any mistake about my view of The Church of Jesus Christ of Latter Day saints. If anything, I feel more strongly now, than I did when I was baptized at age 19, of not only the relevance, but the importance of the church. It is the body that was set in motion by the hand of the Lord through the prophet Joseph Smith. It is authorized by commandment to administer ordinances of the gospel. It has been commanded to preach, teach, exhort, expound.[222] It has been commanded to baptize.[223] It has been commanded to lay on hands for the gift of the Holy Ghost.[224] It has been commanded to bless and pass the sacrament.[225] This is the only church authorized and instructed to perform these rites. If you want to get baptized, then you need to leave the Methodists, Presbyterians, Catholics and even Reverend Lovejoy's Presbylutherans[226] and to come to The Church of Jesus Christ of Latter Day Saints.

Elder Dallin Oaks gave a talk in General Conference in April, 2006, in which he mentioned the continuing presence of the Holy Ghost within the church.[227] All of the examples used in this Conference address were drawn from the experiences of those in the lowest level of the church. It is at the lowest levels of the church

---

[222] See D&C 20:37-60.

[223] D&C 20:37, 72-74.

[224] D&C 20:41.

[225] D&C 20:75-79.

[226] Reverend Lovejoy is a fictional character on *The Simpson's* cartoon. He is a minister in the fictional sect of the Presbylutherans. His fictional faith, however, has as much right to baptize as any other "Christian" denomination, because none of them have been commanded to perform these rites. The Church of Jesus Christ of Latter-day Saints alone has a commission from the Lord to administer these rites.

[227] The talk is titled *All Men Everywhere*, and can be found either online or in the May 2006 *Ensign*.

that I have always lived. And it is in the lowest levels of the church where the Holy Ghost most frequently appears. If you have been on a mission and born testimony of the truthfulness of the Gospel of Jesus Christ, you know this. If you have seen another person convert to the church, you have seen it. You know the hand of God is still over the work going forward in within The Church of Jesus Christ of Latter Day Saints. It will continue to be there as long as we bring the Book of Mormon to the world, and offer them baptism and laying on of hands for the Holy Ghost.

Any of you who choose to preach the Gospel as a missionary in the church in the future will see the hand of God still working among the Saints. But it is my view, and it is my conviction to my core, that if I were to encourage any of you to stop short of pressing forward to finding your Lord, I would risk damnation. I believe such teaching would contradict the invitation extended to every one of you through the prophet Joseph Smith, the Book of Mormon and the revelations contained in the D&C.[228] You read D&C 93:1 and you tell me who has a right to say to you that you should not press forward to see His face and know that He is—not believe, not trust, not hope, but know. *Know* that He is.[229]

There should be an entire chorus of Latter-day Saints who are able to say these words as their own testimony, and not just a quote from the Prophet Joseph Smith: "I had actually seen a light and in the midst of that light I saw two personages and they did in reality speak to me. And though I was hated and persecuted for saying that I had seen a vision yet it was true and while they were persecuting

---

[228] Because of the volume of the information supporting that understanding, I would refer you to *The Second Comforter: Conversing With the Lord Through the Veil* for a full discussion of why I believe this to be true.

[229] Ether 3:16-17.

me and reviling me and speaking all manner of evil against me
falsely for so saying I was lead to say in my heart, Why persecute me
for telling the truth? I have actually seen a vision; and who am I that
I can withstand God, and why does the world think to make me
deny what I have actually seen? For I had seen a vision; I knew it,
and I knew that God knew it, and I could not deny it, neither dared
I do it; at least I knew that by so doing I would offend God, and
come under condemnation." (JS-H 1:25.)

It is not the purpose of the restored gospel to have you get a
testimony of the Book of Mormon, only to then be co-opted into
depending upon anyone other than God for the knowledge of the
truth of all things. Here is the message: "And when you shall receive
these things I would exhort you that you would ask God the Eternal
Father in the name of Christ if these things are not true. If ye shall
ask with a sincere heart, with real intent, having faith in Christ He
will manifest the truth of it unto you by the power of the Holy
Ghost and by the power of the Holy Ghost you may know the
truth of all things." (Moroni 10:4-5.) The truth of *all things*. Not
some, but all.

It is a terrible thing for anyone to presume they can proscribe
your inquiries to God, and limit the scope of truth into which any
of you can inquire and get an answer for yourselves. It is a terrible
responsibility. I would suggest anyone who tries to keep you from
inquiring to know the truth of all things is, like Satan, using fear to
stop your approach to the Being who loves you more than life itself.
He who would gather you as a hen gathers her chicks, if you will
come and be gathered.[230] He would have gathered us and brought
again Zion time after time after time, but *WE* would not. I know
there are people that write books about the future coming of Zion,

---

[230]   See, e.g., 3 Ne. 10:4-6; D&C 43:24-25; Matt. 23:37.

and I know they use quotes from those who think differently than I do. Most of the information in them is really quite unrelated to Zion returning. From the death of Joseph Smith until today, there has not been anything helpful added to what Joseph said on the subject. Although tens-of-thousands of words have been spoken or written about Zion since Joseph's life ended, none of it has brought any closer. If anything, we are further away from it today than we were on June 27, 1844.[231] However, I am not trying to persuade anyone about anything. You are free to believe whatever you want to believe. I only attempt to explain what I believe and why I believe it. You owe it to yourself to investigate these things and ask God yourself about them. I would discourage you from accepting what I, or anyone else, have to say on the subject. Ask God. See if He will not make the matter clear to you.

Perhaps if enough were able to rend the veil of unbelief,[232] there would be reason to send Elijah and begin the final preparatory work. It only takes a few, as we have seen.

With Joseph I testify in the name of Jesus Christ that Elijah will return.

[This paper is based upon a talk given by Denver C. Snuffer, Jr. in October, 2011, but has been corrected, and some content clarified and expanded.]

---

[231] This is the day Joseph and Hyrum were killed.

[232] Ether 4:15.

Essay 3:
Brigham Young's
Telestial Kingdom

Brigham Young's Telestial Kingdom

The Consolidation of Church and State

Summary

Brigham Young's brief tenure (1851-58) as Territorial Governor and Church President allowed him to wield the power of both church and state. How he used this authority reveals much about the man. During the brief reign as God's representative and United States' regent, his sermons reveal how precarious a challenge it presents to consolidate church and state power. His predecessor, Joseph Smith, sought to establish heaven on earth. In contrast, Governor Young had the lesser concern of establishing and operating a "Telestial Kingdom," while aggregating power and making pragmatic decisions in the present world. This article explores Brigham Young's Governorship as a "king's rule," unsuited to the American republic. It includes cautionary advice from the Book of Mormon against attempting this very thing.[233]

Background

Brigham Young was elected president of The Church of Jesus Christ of Latter-day Saints at Winter Quarters in December 1847. Two months later, on February 2, 1848 Mexico signed the treaty of Guadalupe Hidalgo and ceded the Great Basin region to the United States. On March 4, 1849, Brigham Young summoned a convention to draft a constitution for the State of Deseret that he hoped would be approved by the United States Congress. The work of the convention was rapidly completed, the documents drafted, and an election held eight days later. Voters approved the constitution and elected Brigham Young, Governor, his First Counselor, Heber C. Kimball elected Chief Justice, and Second Counselor, Willard Richards elected Secretary of State. All 674 voters approved each of these decisions.

There were discrepancies between the constitutional offices and the slate of elected officers. Further, the constitution set the initial election for "the first Monday of May," not eight days after the convention. The departure from the constitution was because Brigham Young and the Council of Fifty predetermined the outcome. Voters ratified President Young's actions, ignored the constitution, and chose the selected slate in conformity with his wishes. Church Historian Leonard Arrington attributed this discrepancy to "the informal manner in which Brigham and his coterie of associates ran

---

[233] This paper considers Brigham Young's own statements made during the time of his Governorship, and does not cover later statements made after his removal. He learned from his experiences and mistakes, and would later change many of his beliefs because of these experiences. However, those are not relevant to understanding what he believed from 1851-58. For that, I trust in the validity of the Lord's observation: "For of the abundance of the heart his mouth speaketh." Luke 6: 45

things."[234] That particular "informality" was only possible because of the unique roles of Brigham Young.

The Council of Fifty was a shadow government established by Joseph Smith that influenced the thinking of Brigham Young throughout his time as Governor. Therefore, the story of his 1851-1858 Governorship must necessarily begin years prior to Congress establishing the Territory of Utah, and the Presidential appointment of Brigham Young as its first Governor. We must turn back to 1844 when Joseph Smith first organized the Council of Fifty.[235]

The full name of the Council of Fifty was "The Kingdom of God and His Laws with the Keys and Power[s] thereof, and Judgment in the Hands of His Servants, Ahman Christ."[236] The name was too long and therefore was not widely known or regularly used. The two most frequently used names were "The Kingdom of God" or "The Council of Fifty." Today, most Latter-day Saints aware of its existence would recognize it as the "Council of Fifty." However, the early church leaders generally called it "The Kingdom of God" or "The Kingdom."[237] It was the venue where Joseph Smith established his own "Kingship" by being chosen as "our prophet Priest,

---

[234] *Brigham Young, American Moses*, (Alfred A. Knopf, New York, 1985), 224.

[235] The minutes of this Council on April 10, 1880 record the council "was organized by the Lord. April 7th 1842." This is apparently when Joseph Smith first received a revelation about the Council. However, he did not act to establish the Council until March 13, 1844. I use the date of its organization as the commencement date. See D. Michael Quinn, *The Council of Fifty and Its Members, 1844 to 1945*, BYU Studies 20, No. 2 (1980), 2-3. There is some discrepancy on the date of March 13, 1844. Both Wilford Woodruff and Franklin D. Richards state the organization occurred on March 10, 1844. See Quinn, 2, footnote 4, citing *Wilford Woodruff Journal*, 10 March 1844 and *Franklin D. Richards Journal*, 10 April 1880.

236 See Quinn, 3.

[237] Heber C. Kimball and John Henry Smith would use "The Kingdom of God" and Joseph Smith, Willard Richards and Heber C. Kimball would call it "The Kingdom." Quinn, 3-4; also footnotes 12, 13 and 14.

& King by Hosannas."[238] When Joseph Smith spoke in the late-Nauvoo period about "the Kingdom," or "the keys of the Kingdom," he was referring to this council which elevated him to kingship. It was in this council Joseph Smith gave "the keys of the Kingdom" to his inner group of followers to permit them to perpetuate this "Kingdom of God" after his death.

Joseph's kingship anointing culminated the promise of his exaltation. God intends to "exalt" those who were worthy, a status associated with kingship in this life and godhood in the next. The consolidated revelations recorded July 12, 1843[239] state: "Then shall they be gods, because they have no end; therefore shall they be from everlasting to everlasting, because they continue; then shall they be above all, because all things are subject unto them. Then shall they be gods, because they have all power, and the angels are subject unto them."[240]

Joseph lived and died in stratified antebellum America. The nation was divided over slavery. In that setting a religious idea of subservient angels obeying the commands of a worthy and exalted man in a stratified afterlife was easy to grasp and accept. We may find it conceptually hard in post-Civil War/post-Civil Rights America,[241] but Joseph and his contemporaries lived in a differently ordered

---

[238] *William Clayton Journal*, 11 April 1844. By 18 April 1844 the Council was filled. Brigham Young's name was number "23" on the list. William Clayton's description says the list is "of those who have called upon to form the grand K. [Kingdom] of G. [God] by revelation." There were 52 total names listed. *William Clayton Journal* 18 April 1944.

[239] I have discussed the history of this revelation (Section 132) at length in *Passing the Heavenly Gift*, (Mill Creek Press, Salt Lake City, 2011), showing it to be an amalgamation of at least five different revelations beginning in 1829.

[240] D&C 132:20.

[241] For Latter-day Saints perhaps the difficulty may best be reckoned from Official Declaration 2 announced on June 8, 1978. This extended priesthood and Temple blessings to the descendants of former American slaves.

society. The idea that in the afterlife, mankind would be divided into groups of angels who would be subject to and serving more worthy gods was accepted and comfortable to them. To understand their behavior we need to consider their very different world.

Like his predecessor, Brigham Young was ordained a "King, Priest and Ruler over Israel." Though the date of that ordination is not clear,[242] remarks by Governor Young clearly indicate he viewed his status to rule over others as God-given and kingly.[243] This testimony was given by Reynolds Cahoon's son, Bishop Andrew Cahoon, in 1889: "The King of that Kingdom that was set up on the earth was the head of the Church. Brigham Young proclaimed himself King here in Salt Lake Valley before there was a house built, in 1847."[244]

In a sermon delivered on June 19, 1853, two years into his initial term, Governor Young addressed the saints in the Salt Lake Tabernacle as the church president.[245] He explained: "We have got a Territorial Government, and I am and will be Governor, and no power can hinder it, until the Lord Almighty, says, 'Brigham, you need not

---

[242] "Although the exact date of which Brigham Young obtained the theocratic ordination of King, Priest, and Ruler over Israel is not presently known, he undoubtedly received it in the same manner that Joseph Smith did on 11 April 1844 and John Taylor did on 4 February 1885." (Quinn, 18.) On that same page Quinn discusses an account of the John Taylor coronation ceremony, as recorded by Franklin D. Richards.

[243] Given his insistence on being elected church president in 1847, over the active opposition of several other Apostles, it is likely he would not have waited long before receiving the kingship rites, as well. His successor, John Taylor, was elected church president in 1880 and received kingship five years later.

[244] See Klaus J. Hansen, *Quest for Empire, The Political Kingdom of God and The Council of Fifty in Mormon History*, (University of Nebraska Press, Lincoln, 1967), 200 in footnote 74.

[245] The dual nature of his status becomes apparent because Governor Young addressed the church conferences about governmental concerns and the Legislature about religious concerns. The two roles were entirely conflated. This is best understood in the context of a Divine appointment as a "king" which allowed him to move seamlessly in both capacities.

be Governor any longer,' and then I am willing to yield to another Governor."[246]

Arrington's explanation for the "informal manner in which Brigham and his coterie of associates ran things" is best understood against this other, less public Mormon practice. Brigham Young felt comfortable contradicting the draft Territorial constitution because he was a king, and could exercise kingly rule. He called the convention, gave them the mandate, and wanted Territorial recognition from Congress. He knew they would not approve a Rocky Mountain monarchy, and so he at least wanted the appearance of democratic rule. The deviations from what the convention established, and what Brigham Young decreed, gives a glimpse into the difference between Mormonism's public theatre and private reality. A failure to recognize this (or an effort to obscure it) creates a veil which impairs the real view of these events. We cannot understand the conduct if we are not willing to recognize his motivation.

Brigham Young is best understood in the context of his sincere belief he possessed kingship given to him by God. His behavior and sermons reflect the conviction it was a king speaking; those who listened were expected to respond accordingly.

The way the "kingdom" was to function under his leadership is not left unexplained. Brigham Young was the one in control, and he did what he understood Joseph Smith wanted done. He believed ultimately that Jesus was in control, but Brigham was the local, im-

---

[246] *The Complete Discourses of Brigham Young*, Richard S. Van Wagoner editor, (Smith-Pettit Foundation, Salt Lake, 2009) Volume 2, 680 (hereafter *"Complete Discourses"*). All quotes are left uncorrected, as in the original.

mediate leader in charge in this world,[247] and he was following what he understood Joseph Smith wanted done:

> If I could have the desire of my heart I would know precisely the will of Joseph concerning me and how to dictate this people. I do not want to skip Joseph, Peter, Jesus, Moses and go to my Father in Heaven. All I ask for is to be guided by the spirit of Joseph, then let others be governed by their head, or priesthood. Joseph enjoyed the privileges which I never thought I had. Joseph was called of God. I was called of Joseph. I ask you have you ever lost one particle of confidence in me. I do not believe there is one being on earth. Now restore your confidence in yourselves and then in one another, and it casts fear on the minds of the world.[248]

Kingship among gentiles in the Americas is disapproved of in the Book of Mormon. It directs: "[T]his land shall be a land of liberty unto the Gentiles, and there shall be no kings upon this land, who shall raise up unto the Gentiles."[249] Joseph Smith translated the Book of Mormon. Brigham Young was converted because of it. Therefore, we should consider the meaning of this limitation on "kingship."[250] Joseph Smith was anointed "king" before Brigham Young, but Joseph's kingship was entirely theological, private, and non-governmental. His precedent did little to support the form of

---

[247] Brigham Young did not openly call himself "king" in his public statements. This is similar to church presidents not calling themselves "prophets." The title of "prophet" is used by others when referring to the presidents of the church. The presidents themselves have been reluctant to use the term publicly. Similarly, the title of "king" was clearly what Brigham Young claimed beginning in 1847. See footnote 12, supra.

[248] *Complete Discourses*, Vol. 2, 1108, May 25, 1856.

[249] 2 Ne. 10: 11.

[250] The restriction is attributed to "God" (i.e., "this land, saith God," etc.) in 2 Ne. 10: 10-12.

"kingship" implemented by Brigham Young,[251] and far less to justify rebellion against the government.[252]

The earliest events in Utah combined church and state in the person of Brigham Young. Without him, there was no order—social, religious or political. Everything revolved around the church, and after December 1847 the church revolved around him. Colonizer, Governor, Church President, Prophet, Apostle, Lion of the Lord, American Moses, orator, and first citizen; the society of saints were overshadowed by this leader in a way which mirrored, if not exceeded, the way colonial America respected and followed George Washington. Either man could have cut corners, had they elected to do so. In the case of Washington, we have no instance of him doing so. In the case of Brigham Young, however, corners were cut beginning with his election as Governor of an unrecognized territory.[253] President Washington first laid down his authority at the end of the Revolutionary War, and then again after two terms as US President. Brigham Young resisted laying down either of his offices,

---

[251] The first elections in Nauvoo resulted in John C. Bennett elected Mayor. Joseph was also not included in a second tier of City Aldermen. Joseph was elected to the third tier, as a member of the City Council for the Third Ward. John S. Dinger, *The Nauvoo City and High Council Minutes*, (Signature Books, Salt Lake City, 2011), 14.

[252] Rather than retain the weapons when the community was threatened by mobs prior to his death, Joseph surrendered the Nauvoo Legion's rifles to the State of Illinois. Similarly, the Zion's Camp movement from Ohio to Missouri ended without a single shot being fired in hostile action. Joseph disbanded the camp when they faced opposition, and left it to the civil process to sort out the wrongs suffered by his followers.

[253] As we look at his words, we find him using his Governorship while speaking in religious assemblies, and his church presidency while addressing the Legislature. I will note when he spoke as church president and when as Governor. The roles are consistently conflated.

had to be removed as Governor by the US Army, and only surrendered his church position at death.[254]

States have a monopoly on the power to take property, fine, punish, imprison, and even kill its citizens. Brigham Young's religion, however, held no such authority. "[W]e do not believe that any religious society has authority to try men on the right of property or life, to take from them this world's goods, or to put them in jeopardy of either life or limb, or to inflict any physical punishment upon them. They can only excommunicate them from their society, and withdraw from them their fellowship."[255] When analyzing Brigham Young's tenure as Territorial Governor, it is impossible to distinguish between his role as head of state and head of church. Parsing his conduct on the basis of the kind of power used (i.e., the power to punish beyond fellowship) reveals the two roles merged into kingship. The result is a thoroughgoing blend of church and state, where both powers are consistently used simultaneously. Brigham Young ruled as if there were no separation between the two.

When those church members who followed the Quorum of the Twelve were expelled from Nauvoo mid-winter, they governed

---

[254] The LDS church follows the Brigham Young example, and not the most revered Book of Mormon leader, King Benjamin, for succession to the office of church president. King Benjamin surrendered his office and authority when he grew old, rather than holding it until his death as Brigham Young elected. (See Mosiah 1: 9-10.) Similarly, King David surrendered his authority before he died. (1 Kings 1: 33-35.) Nephi also appointed another to be king before his death. (Jacob 1: 9.) The church's structure and legal organization makes passage of the Corporation of the President of the Church of Jesus Christ of Latter-day Saints automatic and only upon death of the senior church apostle.

[255] D&C 134: 10.

themselves through the church.[256] "[C]hurch authorities believed that the Kingdom of God was a political as well as a spiritual kingdom, and that the Priesthood was directly responsible for the effective conduct of civil government."[257] Church revelations clarified to Latter-day Saints that there simply is no distinction between the "temporal" and the "spiritual."[258] The church-in-exile from America had little choice other than to become self-governing. On January 14, 1847 Brigham Young issued his only canonized revelation proclaiming "The Word and Will of the Lord."[259] The opening voice of

---

[256] Less than a year after Joseph and Hyrum's deaths, the Quorum of the Twelve addressed a letter to "the President of the United States of America; To the Governors of the several States; And to the Rulers and People of all Nations" laying out the demand for acknowledgement of God's kingdom. Among other things, the Proclamation demands: "And now, O ye kings, rulers, and people of the Gentiles: hear ye the word of the Lord: for this commandment is for you. You are not only required to repent and obey the gospel in its fullness, and thus become members or citizens of the kingdom of God, but you are also hereby commanded in the name of Jesus Christ, to put your silver and your gold, your ships and steam-vessels, your railroad trains and your horses, chariots, camels, mules, and litters, into active use, for the fulfillment of these purposes. For be it known unto you, that the only salvation which remains for the Gentiles, is for them to be identified in the same covenant, and to worship at the same altar with Israel. In short, they must come to the same standard. For, there shall be one Lord, and his name one, and He shall be king over all the earth." James R. Clark, *Messages of the First Presidency*, (Bookcraft, Salt Lake, 1965), Vol. 1, 255. This Proclamation goes on to explain that God "will assemble the Natives, the remnants of Joseph in America; and make of them a great, and strong, and powerful nation: and he will civilize and enlighten them, and will establish a holy city, and temple, and seat of government among them, which shall be called Zion." *Id.*, 259. These ideas would find their way into later public declarations of Governor Young.

[257] James B. Allen, *Ecclesiastical Influence on Local Government in the Territory of Utah*, Arizona and the West, Vol. 8, No 1 (Spring 1966), 36.

[258] D&C 29: 34-35: "Wherefore, verily I say unto you that all things unto me are spiritual, and not at any time have I given unto you a law which was temporal; neither any man, nor the children of men; neither Adam, your father, whom I created. Behold, I gave unto him that he should be an agent unto himself; and I gave unto him commandment, but no temporal commandment gave I unto him, for my commandments are spiritual; they are not natural nor temporal, neither carnal nor sensual."

[259] This was eleven months prior to him being elected church president.

the revelation is not identified.[260] The voice of Jehovah does not clearly emerge until verse 21. The first 20 verses establish the order for the western exodus, patterned after the 1834 Zion's Camp march from Ohio to Missouri led by Joseph Smith.[261] Church leaders provided the entire leadership structure and government throughout the western migration and first years of settlement.

After the body arrived in the Great Basin, and before the United States provided any recognized appointments, the church filled the void. "The early colonies in Utah were located and settled under the direction of the church leaders. Until counties were fully organized, necessary civil functions in each area were carried out by local bishops and elders. In Provo, for example, a meeting of the 'branch' of the church was held in July of 1849, at which laws were passed imposing fines for gambling with Indians, as well as for shooting in or near the fort."[262] Initially, the only residents were church members. The church had an existing structure capable of governing and the doctrine of the church made no distinction between the temporal and the spiritual. It only made sense the church would provide the structure of both church and state. "[T]he church was in a position to have direct influence on the conduct of county government, for leaders of both institutions were usually the same men; and, because of their ecclesiastical positions, they carried an aura of authority which most settlers respected."[263]

---

[260] It is possible to interpret the first 20 verses as Brigham Young, the Twelve, or Jehovah speaking as "the Lord." The common view is that Jehovah speaks throughout, but it is not until verse 21 that interpretation is clearly established.

[261] See D&C 103: 30-34.

[262] Allen, supra, 37.

[263] Allen, 39.

Despite all the practical reasons, and obvious necessity for the church to step into the void, the distinction between church and state *does* matter. The church was an institution of limited authority, confined to spiritual matters. As we have seen, the scriptures confined it to "fellowship," and never extended into life, property or "this world's goods."[264] The state is another matter.

The power of the state is derived from the right of individuals in a state of nature to punish and retaliate for offenses to the individual. John Locke stated in his *Second Treatise on Civil Government*:

> That, he who has suffered the damage has a right to demand in his own name, and he alone can remit: the damnified person has this power of appropriating to himself the goods or service of the offender, by right of self-preservation, as every man has a power to punish the crime, to prevent its being committed again, by the right he has of preserving all mankind, and doing all reasonable things he can in order to that end: and thus it is, that every man, in the state of nature, has a power to kill a murderer, both to deter others from doing the like injury, which no reparation can compensate, by the example of the punishment that attends it from everybody, and also to secure men from the attempts of a criminal, who having renounced reason, the common rule and measure God hath given to mankind, hath, by the unjust violence and slaughter he hath committed upon one, declared war against all mankind, and therefore may be destroyed as a lion or a tiger, one of those wild savage beasts, with whom men can have no society nor security: and upon this is grounded that great law of nature,

---

[264] "[W]e do not believe that any religious society has authority to try men on the right of property or life, to take from them this world's goods, or to put them in jeopardy of either life or limb, or to inflict any physical punishment upon them. They can only excommunicate them from their society, and withdraw from them their fellowship." (D&C 134: 10.)

Whoso sheddeth man's blood, by man shall his blood be shed. And Cain was so fully convinced, that everyone had a right to destroy such a criminal, that after the murder of his brother, he cries out, Every one that findeth me, shall slay me; so plain was it writ in the hearts of all mankind." (Section 11, spellings have been modernized.)

Locke's and Young's reasoning on the use of state power were similarly respectful of scriptural precedent. But it is difficult to feel the weight of principle when there is an immediate threat to address. When you add to this difficulty the combination of these two forms of power in a single man occupying the head of both church and state, unfortunate results should be expected. The Book of Mormon weighs in and has little to recommend combining the office of "High Priest" over the church with "Chief Judge" over the land. Alma refused it, ceding the power of government to Nephihah and retaining the office of "High Priest over the Church" for himself.[265] Likewise, Joseph Smith, by revelation, gave Hyrum the priesthood and made him co-President, as Joseph assumed the of-

---

[265] Alma 4: 16-20: "And he selected a wise man who was among the elders of the church, and gave him power according to the voice of the people, that he might have power to enact laws according to the laws which had been given, and to put them in force according to the wickedness and the crimes of the people. Now this man's name was Nephihah, and he was appointed chief judge; and he sat in the judgment-seat to judge and to govern the people. Now Alma did not grant unto him the office of being high priest over the church, but he retained the office of high priest unto himself; but he delivered the judgment-seat unto Nephihah. And this he did that he himself might go forth among his people, or among the people of Nephi, that he might preach the word of God unto them, to stir them up in remembrance of their duty, and that he might pull down, by the word of God, all the pride and craftiness and all the contentions which were among his people, seeing no way that he might reclaim them save it were in bearing down in pure testimony against them. And thus in the commencement of the ninth year of the reign of the judges over the people of Nephi, Alma delivered up the judgment-seat to Nephihah, and confined himself wholly to the high priesthood of the holy order of God, to the testimony of the word, according to the spirit of revelation and prophecy."

fice of "king."[266] Unlike Alma, Governor Young chose to remain both with such tenacity that it required an Act of Congress, the United States President acting as Commander in Chief, and the US Army to pry from President Young the Governorship.

One of the first issues facing the provisional Governor and Legislature was property rights. Settlers were building houses, developing farming lots, and distributing water, all of which required a legal framework to provide security for their labors. "[U]ntil it took steps in this direction the people could obtain not title to their homes. Much anxiety was felt by them in consequence. While waiting for the National Government to dispose of the soil, the Provisional Government made temporary grants to its citizens, of the lands they occupied, including the use of grazing ground, with water and timber for milling and lumbering purposes."[267] These temporary measures were necessarily undertaken, and had the effect of promoting community development and reaffirming the authority of the church and its leaders. The resulting level of fidelity to these community benefactors is difficult for us to understand from our vantage point. The lives of the citizens were utterly dependent upon the good graces of the church. The inevitable result elevated Governor Brigham Young in the hearts and minds of his followers.

The Territorial government's provisional application to become a United States Territory was not without controversy. Debate lasted for nearly a year in the US Senate. When finally passed, President Millard Fillmore signed the bill on September 9, 1850 and appointed Brigham Young the first Territorial Governor of the Territory of

---

[266] See D&C 124: 91 (giving Priesthood) and 94-95 (making him prophet to the church). *William Clayton's Journal* records on July 16, 1843 Joseph said the following: "Hyrum held the office of prophet to the church by birthright... the Saints must regard Hyrum for he has authority."

[267] Orson F. Whitney, *Popular History of Utah*, (Deseret News Press, Salt Lake, 1916), 66.

Utah. Although appointed in September, the news did not arrive in Utah until January 27, 1851.[268] Brigham Young was touring northern settlements and did not hear until the next day. He was officially sworn into the office of Territorial Governor on February 3, 1851. "Brigham Young, Governor of Deseret by popular vote, was now Governor of Utah by presidential appointment[.]"[269]

The "Act to Establish a Territorial Government for Utah" included in Section 2, the following language:

> That the executive power and authority in and over said Territory of Utah shall be vested in a governor, who shall hold his office for four years, and until his successor shall be appointed and qualified,[270] unless sooner removed by the President of the United States. The governor shall preside within said Territory, shall be commander-in-chief of the militia thereof, shall perform the duties and receive the emoluments of superintendent of Indian affairs, and shall approve all laws passed by the legislative assembly before they shall take effect: he may grant pardons for offenses against the laws of said Territory, and reprieves for offenses against the laws of the United States, until the decision of the President can be made known thereon; he shall commission all officers who shall be appointed to office under

---

[268] The appointment was reported in the *New York Tribune*, which found its way to San Francisco. Returning missionary Henry E. Gibson brought a copy of the newspaper with him when he returned to Salt Lake. In the paper was a list of appointments, including Brigham Young's. (*Id*, 72, and footnote found there.) The church and Territory learned of the appointment through the *Fifth General Epistle Of the Presidency of the Church of Jesus Christ of Latter-day Saints*, dated April 7, 1851. The letter can be found in James R. Clark, *Messages of the First Presidency*, (Bookcraft, Salt Lake City, 1965), Vol. 2, 62-73.

[269] Orson F. Whitney, supra, 72. Interestingly, although the church's First Presidency acknowledged the Act of Congress established the Territory of "Utah," the church continued to refer to "citizens of Deseret" in correspondence. See James R. Clark, supra, Vol. 2, 68, 74.

[270] He was appointed to a four year term, but served seven years because a replacement was not made until Alfred Cumming was appointed by President James Buchanan.

the laws of the said Territory, and shall take care that the laws be faithfully executed.[271]

The US Government granted rights that only confirmed the existing reality. It was a politically astute move by President Fillmore. Brigham Young's and Utah's appreciation is reflected in naming Millard County and Fillmore City as a tribute to him.

On June 15, 1851 the two roles merge. When speaking about horse theft and Indians, Brigham Young said, (after explaining Indians are taught to steal from birth and whites were taught not to steal): "[W]hile they are in their degraded state, it rests upon us to use wisdom and judgment in their behalf. I say to the Saints, kill every white man you see stealing and not kill the Indian for it, for the white men know better. I speak to the Saints not as the Governor of Utah, but you and I are sent to save Israel not to kill them."[272] He spoke of killing (an impermissible penalty for the church). The audience was "the Saints," and yet he stressed he did not speak as "Governor of Utah." Six days later he told the Saints: "[W]e are a kingdom and must bring the kingdom in subject to the will of God."[273] He conflated the two, because President/Governor Young led both simultaneously.

President Young gave a definition of "liberty" in a sermon on June 29, 1851, some of which reads like John Locke:

> The spirit of liberty is the spirit of submission. If you wish to enjoy liberty in your fullness you must submit to the rule to the land of liberty. The privilege of living in liberty to all eternity adopt every holy principle and gather together

---

[271] 31st Congress, Session 1, Chapter 51, 1850, *Act to provide a Territorial Government for Utah*, September 9, 1850.

[272] *Complete Discourses*, Vol. 1, 434.

[273] *Id.*, 436, June 22, 1851.

every thing on earth and make you happy… You are not at liberty to infringe on the rights of your neighbors. If a man injure me, I am at liberty to make him pay for it. Every person in heaven is at liberty when they have the privilege to organize a kingdom for themselves, but unless they are submissive to their presidents on earth, they never can have the privilege to the last day of eternity. If they are faithful here, they will be make gods in eternity.[274]

Submission to "their presidents on earth," meaning church leaders, was the price of godhood in eternity. Liberty meant "submission" to the king and the prize for submitting to the earthly president will be eternal godhood. This was the motivation for his followers. They were willing to be his subjects here in the hope of becoming something godlike hereafter.

Governor Young did not believe that Mormon governance was limited to the Great Basin. He explained: "All things will have to bow to Mormonism or eternal light and truth. We have the true government of all the earth."[275] If Mormonism had the right to govern "all the earth" and Brigham Young was its earthly king, then it follows there should be no conceptual end of his kingdom.[276]

President Young wanted his kingdom to be self-sufficient. Therefore, he did not want his believers to buy from non-Mormon suppliers. "Everything is against Mormonism and Mormonism is against everything. Everything is against us. Hear it, O earth, for the Kingdom of God is against all earth and hell. This is true and we shall fight them until the kingdom of this world becomes the kingdom of our God. We shall fight battle after battle until the victory is

---

[274] *Id.*, 440.

[275] *Id.*, 448.

[276] Compare Isaiah 9: 7: "Of the increase of his government and peace there shall be no end."

won; we have to fight and lay down our lives for Christ's sake."[277]
The rhetoric was overwrought, and the impressions left were undoubtedly significant. The "battles" underway in 1851 were anything
but violent. The political appointment of non-Mormon judges by
Washington was unacceptable to Utah, and Utah's social structure
was unacceptable to them. These hostile judges intended to return
to Washington and raise political opposition to Utah's (and therefore
the church's) leaders.

Fiery rhetoric from Brigham Young was commonplace. Initially
it was more alarming in tone than in effect. However, continuing
fiery rhetoric combined with deteriorating environmental circumstances did finally result in unfortunate events which were only possible because church and state merged in Brigham Young.

In January 1852, Governor Young spoke to the Legislature
about slavery, sin and punishment. Borrowing from the Law of
Moses, he declared: "The time will come, that if a man will take the
name of God in vain, he will be hewn down without judgment or
trial!"[278] He added: "The time will also come when if the parents are
sanctified before the Lord, and their children rise up in disobedience
against them, they will be hewn down."[279] This talk discussed a

---

[277] *Id.*, 461, October 6, 1851.

[278] *Id.*, 466, January 4, 1852.

[279] *Id.*

topic that is still controversial.[280] He advanced the idea a man must be killed for his own sins by shedding his blood:[281]

> In the days of ancient Israel, justice was dealt out in a manner that showed they understood principle, and revered the commandments of God. It was a mercy to many to have justice and judgment executed upon them on the Earth, even to be slain and have their blood poured out upon the Earth, that it might be tolerable for them. God made a covenant with Abraham and his seed, that He would save them. When they committed sin, He slew them, that He might save them, by their spilling their blood as an offering. Had they lived in sin, they might have sinned so as not to have been forgiven or saved. It was mercy to slay them.[282]

The next day he added: "It is the greatest blessing that could come to some men to shed their blood on the ground, and let it come up before the Lord as an atonement."[283] Brigham Young, as king, thought it his burden to create righteous people from those over whom he held authority, even if it required some to die to ac-

---

[280] He also spoke in this address about Negros being descended from Cain, their lineage being cursed, and therefore, denied priesthood, and that intermarriage with descendants of Cain justified execution of both parties. However, that issue is beyond the scope of this paper.

[281] This was not altogether original to Brigham Young. Joseph Smith responded to a Nauvoo City debate over hanging by stating his preference for shooting or cutting the throat of an offender: "In debate on the bill, Geo[rge] A. Smith thought imprisonment better than hanging. Mayor [Joseph Smith] said he was opposed to hanging. If a man kill another[,] shoot him[,] or cut his throat[,] spilling his blood on the ground[,] and let the smoke thereof ascend up to God. If I ever have the privilege of Making a law on this point[,] I will have it so." Scott H. Faulring, ed., *An American Prophet's Record: The Diaries and Journals of Joseph Smith*, (Signature Books, Salt Lake City, 1989), 326-28. Brigham Young's advocacy greatly expanded the idea beyond Joseph Smith's desire to see capital punishment result in blood being spilled in the Nauvoo City debate.

[282] *Complete Discourses*, Vol. 1, 467, January 4, 1857.

[283] *Id.*, 469

complish it.[284] As Commander in Chief of the Territorial Militia he could use military force, and he could invite the Legislature to pass laws which included the death penalty.[285] A few years later this kind of rhetoric would bring about the Mormon Reformation, which was the beginning of the end for his Governorship.

In an address to the two houses of the Legislature on January 29, 1852, he commented: "we find it is a hard matter to enact human laws to govern a divine kingdom."[286] The Governor and church president, or 'priest and king,' saw the challenge in these terms. They were stewards over "human laws," but he was steward over "a divine kingdom." The solution to the challenge, he explained to the Legislature, was to "draw out from the laws which God has given for His divine Kingdom. And make enactments to control all people, to a certain extent under the divine control of His own Kingdom on Earth, this I also believe."[287] To clarify that his ambition was not limited to the Territory of Utah, but would expand to dominate the whole world, Governor Young declared:

> For as the Lord lives, and as this people lives, they have this to do sooner or later. They have to usher forth their enactments, to govern the Jews and the Gentiles, and all the nations which are included with Israel, and with the Gentiles, that every professed Christian, every religious denomination, and every government under the whole heaven may

---

[284] Mormon scripture also disapproved coerced behavior, even if the object was to "save" souls. See, e.g., Moses 4:1-3.

[285] For a discussion about Utah's legacy of capital punishment see Martin R. Gardner, *Mormonism and Capital Punishment: A Doctrinal Perspective, Past and Present*, Dialogue: A Journal of Mormon Thought, Vol. 12, No. 1, Spring 1989, 9-26.

[286] *Complete Discourses*, Vol. 1, 475, January 29, 1852.

[287] *Id.*

find shelter under this broad banner which shall be spread over them by the Lord Almighty. That I also believe.[288]

If God owns this world, then His Kingdom ought to rule over all of it. The scope is necessarily universal. This cosmic reach reflected the Governor's religious convictions. As he concluded his remarks he declared: "Jehovah is my king. I care not what can be said to the contrary. The Lord Jehovah is my king and instructor, and I wish you to serve Him. That is the way I would do it if I was in the Legislature[.]"[289]

Non-Mormon federal appointees left Utah and accused Governor Young of being a dictator. Brigham Young thought he had the right to dictate. He was not limited by traditional American constraints. He answered to a much higher authority. His response revealed that he thought his prerogative reckoned from God and the Council of Fifty. His status was given by God:

> I am accused by our honorable judges who have left this Territory last fall of entering into the Legislative Hall and there dictating them. That is an objection that will be raised and will be presented to President Fillmore; that I entered into the Halls of Legislature and there dictate them. I do dictate and I never expect to see the day while I am Governor amongst this people that I don't do it, and I want it published abroad for it is what I believe in, and it is what you believe in…I want these Gentlemen to realize, to be fully sensible of, is simply this; that when they meet here in a legislative capacity, not to forget that they are Elders in Israel, Apostles of the Lord Jesus Christ, that they are Saints of the Most High God, and I hope and pray that a feeling to the contrary of this may never arise in the bosom

---

[288]   *Id.*

[289]   *Id.*, 476.

of anyone of these men...[Referring to pre-Territorial days]We then legislated for the benefit of the inhabitants of the State of Deseret. The most of them belonged to the council that is called the Council of Fifty.[290]

Reflecting on the possibility the he could be removed as Governor by President Fillmore, he added: "They may send another governor here, but I shall govern the people by the Eternal Priesthood of the Son of God."[291]

At the end of the next month, the Legislature threw a social party. The Governor addressed the party. In his lengthy remarks, he reflected on the difficult burden he carried to be everyone's constant adviser. He recommended physical labor for its health benefits, and then declared he couldn't cut wood or hoe a garden because he was constantly interrupted by someone wanting counsel. He declared, "I have given it up, I do not intend to work any more at manual labor."[292] He explained to them how he knew they were God's chosen Kingdom on Earth. "When you see all the powers of the evil one combined against a community, you may know that is Christ's kingdom. Everything has proved that this is God's kingdom."[293] In other words, positive proof of God's favor can be found in resistance and opposition from anywhere. Governor Young detected universal proof of God's favor.

President Young addressed the General Conference a month later, and expounded on how every man's property should be bound

---

[290] *Id.*, 476-77, February 4, 1852.

[291] *Id.* 477.

[292] *Id.*, 485, March 4, 1852. This notion the ruler is spared manual labor for his own support is contrary to the kingship model of King Benjamin. See Mosiah 2:12-19.

[293] *Id.*, 487.

to the church. He wanted it so that if a man wanted to apostatize from the religion their economic survival prevented it:

> If any man is in darkness through the deceitfulness of riches, it is good policy for him to bind up his wealth in this Church, so that he cannot command it again, and he will be apt to cleave to the kingdom. If a man has the purse in his pocket, and he apostatizes, he takes it with him; but if his worldly interest is firmly united to the Kingdom of God, when he arises to go away, he finds the calf is bound, and, like the cow, he is unwilling to forsake it. If his calf is bound up here, he will be inclined to stay; all his interest is here, and ever likely the Lord will open his eyes, so that he will properly understand his true situation, and his heart will chime in with the will of his God in a very short time. Were we to dedicate our moral and intellectual influence, and our earthly wealth to the Lord, our hearts would be very likely to applaud our acts. This reasoning is for those who do not feel exactly to subscribe to all that has been said this morning, with regard to dedicating ourselves to the cause of truth. This is what you must do to obtain an exaltation. The Lord must be first and foremost in our affections, the building of His kingdom demands our first consideration.[294]

President Young envisioned merging Saint to church, church to state, and himself in control of it all. One great beehive, united and working for one purpose: to support the king's efforts to further his King's will. There was something much bigger going on for Brigham Young. He had a grander purpose: "The Millennium consists in this—every heart in the Church and Kingdom of God being united in one; the Kingdom increasing to the overcoming of every-

---

[294] *Id.*, 491, April 6, 1852.

thing opposed to the economy of heaven, and Satan being bound."[295]

In the words of Brigham Young, there is a seamless harmony between it all. But the seamlessness requires us to view it the same as did he. Until you recognize his kingship, you don't see what the Governor was trying to accomplish.

On August 29, 1852 the private practice of having plural wives was made public. As church president he spoke after the announcement and declared:

> [I]t will sail over and ride triumphantly above all the prejudice and priestcraft of the day; it will be fostered and believed in by the more intelligent portion of the world as one of the best doctrines ever proclaimed to any people. Your hearts need not beat; you need not think that a mob is coming here to tread upon the sacred liberty which the Constitution of our country guarantees unto us, for it will not be.[296]

He then quoted an unidentified US Senator[297] who advised in favor of this public disclosure, suggesting it would be something the entire country would welcome as an advantage to public health. The expected public acceptance never happened. Nor did the principle ultimately receive Constitutional vindication. Those matters, however, were not resolved until long after Brigham Young's Governorship.

Criticism from all sides continued to mount against Governor Young from the national press, as well as from dissidents and non-

---

[295]   *Id.*

[296]   *Id.* 582, August 29, 1852.

[297]   Stephen A. Douglas was the unnamed source.

Mormons. In an October address to the church, President Young declared how futile it was to consider removing him as Governor:

> What says the United States? "Let us send a governor there; let us send our judges there." But what do they cry? "We have no influence or power, for there are other men there who rule, and we cannot help it; they have the reins of government and turn the people whithersoever they will, and we cannot help ourselves." What did a gentleman say to Mr. Fillmore? Said he, "You need not send anybody there, for Brigham Young is Governor, and he will govern the people all the time; and there is no other man that can govern them." If there is any truth in this, it is, he will do so as long as the Lord lets him.[298]

It is apparent President Brigham Young said exactly what he meant. Later events, including removing him from power over the state, the abolition of plural marriage, domestication of the church by the nation, all influence the way Mormons now interpret the words of Brigham Young. Consider for a moment these words in their literal meaning: "How are this people to be ruled, to be dictated in their future course. The Lord Almighty had built up his kingdom, here is the church and kingdom of the Lord God Almighty upon the earth. This is the kingdom [the church] to this kingdom [the world]."[299]

Five days later, another preview of a coming Reformation appears in his conference address. Speaking of those who killed Joseph Smith, including the governor and militia who were involved, Brigham Young said, "[if they] had come and had us to cut off their heads and let their blood be shed on the ground to atone for their

---

[298] *Complete Discourses, supra,* Vol. 1., 591, October 3,1852.

[299] *Id.* 595.

sin. The nation might have redeemed themselves, if they had taken those murderers and spilt their blood, but they have held their peace."[300] The result, he declared, would require innocent blood to be shed in their place, for the nation to wipe their sin away.[301]

In June 1853, President Young addressed a church conference complaining of Judge Brocchus, the Territorial judge appointed by the federal government who abandoned his position and returned to Washington to complain. "It is true, as it is said in the Report of these officers, if I had crooked my little finger, he would have been used up, but I did not bend it."[302] He conceded he has the power to 'use up' a critic by the smallest of gestures, and noted that he refrained. However, he went on to caution "apostates, or men who never have made any profession of religion, had better be careful how they come here, lest I should bend my little finger."[303] Protecting his kingdom from internal apostasy or waywardness was another matter. He could be provoked into action by anything he suspected as apostasy.

In this talk, President Young again remarked about his right to remain as head of state:

> "I have no fears whatever of Franklin Pierce excusing me from office, and saying that another man shall be the Governor of this territory." He explained some of the history of getting the Territory recognized, remarking that he told the original delegation "I will be Governor still, after you have done every thing you possibly can do to prevent it." It was his right. God, and the Council of Fifty, had made him

---

[300] *Id.*, 596.

[301] This is an early harbinger of the events later played out at Mountain Meadows.

[302] *Complete Discourses*, Vol. 2, 680, June 19, 1853.

[303] *Id.*

king. Therefore, "We have got a Territorial Government, and I am and will be Governor, and no power can hinder it, until the Lord Almighty says, 'Brigham, you need not be Governor any longer,' and then I am willing to yield[.]"[304]

The Governor's Reformation

With that background we turn to the Mormon Reformation. By 1856, Willard Richards had died (March 11, 1854) and was replaced by Jedediah M. Grant in the First Presidency of the church. Brigham Young had been Governor for five years. Political conditions were complicated by increased criticism both in the Territory, and the nation. Plural wives, as expected, had not been welcomed. The kingdom was struggling. A new national political party was emerging whose popularity was driven by its opposition to both slavery and polygamy.

Beginning in 1855, in addition to political and social difficulties, President Young was confronted by natural disasters. "The first major calamity was a grasshopper plague. On April 30, 1855 Brigham Young noted that 'grasshoppers have made their appearance and a doing extensive damage.'"[305] A drought was underway, and the plague added to crop losses. Food became scarce. "The drought was followed by a severe winter. In an effort to find more suitable grazing, it was decided to move many cattle, including more of the church herd, northward to Cache Valley. Biting snow and extreme cold soon proved this to be an unwise decision, and the loss in stock was extensive. Brigham estimated that two-thirds of all church stock had perished, while Wilford Woodruff recorded that only five hundred

---

[304] *Id.*

[305] Paul H. Peterson, *The Mormon Reformation of 1856-1857: The Rhetoric and the Reality*, Journal of Mormon History,, Vol. 15, 1989, 62, (citing Brigham Young's letter to John Taylor, April 30, 1855, *Brigham Young Letterbooks*, LDS Church Archives, Salt Lake City, Utah).

cattle remained from a herd of twenty-six hundred."[306] The winter
of 1855-56 was another catastrophe atop the already direful circumstances. The January and February 1856 deep snow killed cattle they
could ill afford to lose. Not only were cattle lost in Cache Valley, but
horses also. Conditions required them to be kept in barns and fed
hay to survive. By spring, two-thirds of all the livestock had died.[307]
The entire kingdom was threatened. These disasters "in one year,
wiped out the entire social surplus and placed the 35,000 persons in
the territory in the same position of semi-starvation in which the
early Salt Lake colonists found themselves before the Gold
Rush."[308] How was the king to view a kingdom that had been re-
buked by nature's God? Where was the blame to be placed?[309] What
was to be done?

Although there were two explanations for these calamities,
Brigham Young apparently only considered one. Either the leaders
had brought this onto the kingdom, or the subjects had failed.
Someone had offended God and needed to repent. Of the two al-
ternatives, President Young chose to blame the subjects. What followed was a "Mormon Reformation" designed to "rekindle faith
and testimony throughout the Church."[310] This period is, to say the
least, still controversial. It excites extravagant claims by critics and
brings out equally extravagant apologies from church defenders. A

---

[306] *Id.*, 63.

[307] See Polly Aird, *Mormon Convert, Mormon Defector: A Scottish Immigrant in the American West, 1848-1861*, (Arthur H. Clark, Norman Oklahoma, 2009), 156; citing *Millennial Star* 18 (June 21, 1856): 396-97; Arrington, *Great Basin Kingdom*, 125-136.

[308] Arrington, *Great Basin Kingdom*, 148.

[309] "Gentile conflicts, assimilation problems, difficulties with apostates, and especially natural disasters, all implied that the Lord was not happy with the atmosphere in Mor-mondom." (Paul H. Peterson, 63.)

[310] *Encyclopedia of Mormonism*, Vol. 3, 1197, "Reformation (LDS) Of 1856-1857."

dispassionate view is difficult, if not impossible. Here is a semi-official[311] explanation for the controversy:

> The era of the Reformation is often regarded as a contro-versial period. Some critics have claimed that Blood Atonement was practiced at this time. While President Young did preach that forgiveness for certain sins could come only through the sinner's shedding his blood, such comments reflect his style more than his intent. Many of Brigham Young's utterances were rhetorical and designed to encourage (or even frighten) Saints into gospel confor-mity. While publicly he threatened, privately he instructed Church leaders to forgive those who expressed sorrow for sin and repented.[312]

Here is a contrary view by Polly Aird, which begins by quoting Peter McAuslan:

> "With all their [the Mormons'] honesty, they have often been led to do wrong, even to the taking of the lives of their fellows. This I know by my experience in Utah. Two prominent instances of such you will remember of when I mention the names of the places at which they occurred, Springville and Mountain Meadows."

George A. Hicks, to whom Peter reported in the Nauvoo Legion, wrote later that in this period "a spirit of secret

[311] *The Encyclopedia of Mormonism* was prepared by an editorial board consisting of recognized Mormon scholars. It included, from Brigham Young University, Daniel H. Ludlow, Robert J. Matthews, Charles D. Tate, Jr., Robert K. Thomas, Stan L. Albrecht, S. Kent Brown, Ronald K. Esplin, Truman G. Madsen, Terrance D. Olson, Larry C. Porter, Noel B. Reynolds, and John W. Welch; from the University of Utah, Addie Fuhriman, and from Columbia University Richard L. Bushman. None of these individuals could speak "officially" for the church. However, they represent at least the best thinking of Mormonism's academic community. An "official" position for the church is a challenge few have solved. See the FAIR prepared article titled *"What is 'Official' LDS Doctrine?"* at www.fairlds.org/wp-content/uploads/2012/02/What_is_Mormon_Doctrine.pdf as one recent effort.

[312] *Complete Discourses*, Vol. 2, 1197, November 30, 1856.

murder stalked abroad among the people, and many of the 'undesirables' lost their lives by being murdered by unknown assassins, unknown so far as the general public were concerned." And Peter wrote, "I know from my experience in Mormonism that to give it [the church] the power it would rewrite the world's history with the blood of its inhabitants. This you may think is strong language but it is in accord with the spirit of the leaders of the Mormon Church when I was in Utah."[313]

The first explanation is drawn largely from Mormon academics employed by the church. They are obligated to the institution responsible for the events. Their description relies on characterizations and subjective interpretation, and their natural sympathies for their employer is understandable.

When choosing between these two opposing views, even though it is biting, the second appears more accurate. Polly Aird took statements from those who lived through the events. She is non-Mormon, but not anti-Mormon, and she can report what she thinks true without being accused of faithlessness. Faithful Mormons like me are often regarded as weak in the faith if they are both believing and honest. Even church leaders sometimes find church history so disturbing they prefer it advocated by apologists. But human failure does not make any religion false. I do not believe shortcomings by those who practice my faith can ever damage it.

Governor/President Young's rhetoric, which followed the trials of 1855-56, blamed the subjects of his kingdom for the judgments of God. Something needed to be done to appease an angry Deity. Here are excerpts from his March 2, 1856 address, given as the

---

[313]   Aird, 219-220; footnotes omitted.

kingdom was emerging from that difficult winter, facing starvation again in the early spring:

> [L]et me say to the Latter-day Saints that they stand upon slippery places. They do not all fully know the paths they walk in, they do not all perfectly understand their own ways and doings, many do not altogether realize their own weaknesses, do not understand the power of the devil and how liable they are to be decoyed one hair's breadth, to begin with, from the line of truth. They are first drawn by a fine line, in a little time it becomes a cord, it soon increases to a strong rope, and from that to a cable; thus it grows from the size of a spider's web, in comparison.
>
> Let a Saint diverge from the path of truth and rectitude, in the least, no matter in what, it may be in a deal with his neighbor, in lusting after that which is not in his possession, in neglecting his duty, in having an over anxiety for something he should not be anxious about in being a little distrustful with regard to the providences of God, *in entertaining a misgiving in his heart and feeling with regard to the hand of the Lord towards him, and his mind will begin to be darkened...*
>
> If there is a misgiving in the heart with regard to confidence in our God, do you not see that there is a chance for one to slide a hair's breadth from the truth? ...
>
> I will tell you what this people need, with regard to preaching; you need, figuratively, to have it rain pitchforks, tines downwards, from this pulpit, Sunday after Sunday. Instead of the smooth, beautiful, sweet, still, silk-velvet-lipped preaching, *you should have sermons like peals of thunder, and perhaps we then can get the scales from our eyes...*
>
> I know the condition of this people, I know what induces them to do as they do, I know the secret springs to their actions, how they are beset, the temptations and evils that

are around them, and how liable they are to be drawn away, consequently, *I tell you, brethren, that you need to have the thunders of the Almighty and the forked lightnings of truth sent upon you, to wake you up out of your lethargy...*

[I]f the kingdom of God is on the earth it is here, ... The people should be preached to, but they need something besides smooth teaching. Comparatively speaking, they should have their ears cuffed and be roughly handled, be kicked out doors, and then kicked in again. Most of the Elders who preach in this stand ought to be kicked out of it, and then kicked into it again, until they overhaul themselves and find out what is the matter with them...

Do you not know that you need the Spirit of the Almighty to look through a man and discern what is in his heart, while his face smiles upon you and his words flow as smoothly as oil? *If you had the power of God upon you, you might see the sword lurking within him, and that, if he had the power, he would plunge it in your heart and destroy you from the earth.* I meet many such men in these streets, and in the houses round about...

The time is coming when justice will be laid to the line and righteousness to the plummet; when we shall take the old broad sword and ask, "Are you for God?" and if you are not heartily on the Lord's side, you will be hewn down. I feel like reproving you; you are like a wild ass that rears and almost breaks his neck before he will be tamed. It is so with this people...

You may expect the best and worst of all God's creation mingled here together. The foolish will turn from correct principles, go over to the wicked, and cease to be righteous, so that they can go to hell with the fools.[314]

---

[314] *Complete Discourses*, Vol. 2, 1058-1061, March 2, 1856, emphasis added.

To understand how direful circumstances were at the time, fourteen days later President Young advised members of his kingdom to go no more than five days without eating something.[315] His followers were severely suffering. He made the diagnosis and prescribed the cure: Thorough, severe and complete repentance needed to happen, and the kingdom's leaders needed to cause it.[316] In other words, Mormonism needed to be reformed. Repentance needed to be significant enough to remove God's ire. Brigham Young intended to set that in motion using fiery rhetoric and, failing that, fiery enforcement.

As to his status as kingdom leader, he continued in his confidence that the hand of God upheld him.[317] Therefore, any anger he provoked from the US government was inconsequential:

I shall be Governor as long as the Lord Almighty wishes me to govern this people.

Do you suppose that it is in the power of any man to thwart the doings of the Almighty? They may as well undertake to blot out the sun. I am in the hands of that God, so is the President of our nation, and so are kings, and emperors, and all rulers. He controls the destiny of all, and what are you and I going to do about it? Let us submit to

---

[315] *Id.*, 1070, March 16, 1856.

[316] The clear thinking of where responsibility lay for these problems is shown in Apostle Pratt's remarks during that snowy February: "One calamity after another, one punishment after another...Will it not learn us a lesson? ...O Lord, let thy chastening hand be upon this people, until they learn to obey those good and wholesome counsels that are poured out from this stand by those who preside over us." Orson Pratt, *Journal of Discourses*, Vol. 3, 297, February 10, 1856.

[317] In the many public talks during this period, I found no suggestion he questioned whether he had done or was doing something offensive to God. If he did, it was concealed from public view.

Him, that we may share in this invisible, almighty, God-like power, which is the everlasting Priesthood.[318]

The subjects of the kingdom needed to be purged. If they were unwilling or unable to conform to the demands of righteousness, then they would need to be cut off like a dead branch. Clearing away these dead branches would only benefit the remainder:

[M]ercy is not always to be extended to the people, judgment must claim its right.

If we wish this Church and kingdom of God upon the earth, to be like a find, healthy, growing tree, we should be careful not to let the dead branches remain too long...

When we have learned that they are really dead, then there is danger in suffering them to remain too long, for they will begin to decay and tend to destroy the tree. When we are satisfied that a limb is dead we clip it off close to the trunk, and cover up the wound that it may not cause any more injury...

[D]isfellowship them, and let them know that they must observe the laws of this kingdom, or eventually be cut off.[319]

During this time, to show their increased zeal, the entire Utah Legislature was rebaptized as an official act.[320] The purpose of the rhetoric of the Reformation was twofold: Either increased devotion to the kingdom, or scare all disloyal subjects into fleeing. The Utah Legislature increased devotion. Hundreds fled.

---

[318] *Complete Discourses*, Vol. 2, 1070, March 16, 1856.

[319] *Complete Discourses*, Vol. 2, 1072-73, March 23, 1856.

[320] Ardis E. Parshall, *Pursue, Retake and Punish: The 1857 Santa Clara Ambush*, Utah Historical Quarterly, Winter 2005, Vol. 73, No. 1, 68.

By September 1856, Jedediah Grant was preaching "Reformation." In the Reformation, Brigham Young linked killing sinners and salvation together. Here is one of his earliest sermons on the subject which was reported in the *Deseret News*, spread throughout the Territory, and repeated in national newspapers:

> There are sins that men commit for which they cannot receive forgiveness in this world, or in that which is to come, and if they had their eyes open to see their true condition, they would be perfectly willing to have their blood spilt upon the ground, that the smoke thereof might ascend to heaven as an offering for their sins; and the smoking incense would atone for their sins, whereas, if such is not the case, they will stick to them and remain upon them in the spirit world.

> I know, when you hear my brethren telling about cutting people off from the earth, that you consider it is strong doctrine; but it is to save them, not to destroy them.[321]

According to Governor Young, it was an act of Christian charity to kill. Indeed, the more enlightened could see the value of killing the wicked for the purpose of saving them:

> I know that there are transgressors, who, if they knew themselves, and the only condition upon which they can obtain forgiveness, would beg of their brethren to shed their blood, that the smoke thereof might ascend to God as an offering to appease the wrath that is kindled against them, and that the law might have its course. I will say further; I have had men come to me and offer their lives to atone for their sins.[322]

---

[321] *Complete Discourses*, Vol. 2, 1169-1170, September 21, 1856.

[322] *Id.*

Rhetoric has consequences. "As with any reform movement, there were problems, excesses, and improprieties."[323] This kind of language has been excused by many Mormon apologists, who recognize this highly charged language requires some explanation. However, less than a year later the Mountain Meadows Massacre happened in the southern part of the kingdom. There was a connection between rhetoric and killing.

The Encyclopedia of Mormonism states: "Many of Brigham Young's utterances were rhetorical and designed to encourage (or even frighten) Saints into gospel conformity."[324] The recent book co-authored by Assistant LDS Church Historian Richard Turley states: "From Young's perspective, the reformation accomplished a great deal of good, though tough talk about blood atonement and dissenters must have helped create a climate of violence in the territory, especially among those who chose to take license from it."[325] D. Michael Quinn observes: "Despite the suffering imposed by anti-Mormons on them, despite hearing repeated sermons about blood atonement, despite singing hymns of vengeance, despite receiving patriarchal blessings promising them the privilege of taking revenge on their enemies, the historical evidence indicates that most early Mormons avoided violence and were saddened by the news of such incidents." By 1890, when the abandonment of polygamy made statehood at last possible, Mormonism reached a point of "abandonment of its violent culture and the beginning of its selective memory of a turbulent past."[326] Paul H. Peterson explained, "[A]s

---

[323]   Paul H. Peterson, 72.

[324]   *Encyclopedia of Mormonism*, Vol. 3, 1197.

[325]   Ronald Walker, Richard Turley Jr., and Glen Leonard, *Massacre at Mountain Meadows: An American Tragedy.* (Oxford University Press, Oxford, 2008), 25-27.

[326]   D. Michael Quinn, *Mormon Hierarchy: Extensions of Power*, (Signature Books, Salt Lake City, 1997), 260-61.

the Reformation progressed, it became clear to the church leaders that not all would reform and that community purity would never become a reality until all polluting elements were removed. Thus, getting rid of incorrigibles came to be nearly as important as purifying those who were earnest in their desire to do better."[327]

There is not yet enough distance between events and emotions to allow dispassionate history by faithful Mormons to be accepted. Moreover, once the church abandons a practice, the mention or memory of these past practices is removed from the institution as the new view is adopted.[328] This is a challenge for faithful Mormons who would like to better understand their faith's history. Perhaps the recent work of Richard L. Bushman signals the possibility of change.[329] The single most violent episode of the era still tears at the community. The sole party executed for the Mountain Meadows Massacre, John D. Lee, was posthumously reinstated to full church

---

[327]   Paul H. Peterson, 73.

[328]   During the candidacy of B.H. Roberts for Congress in 1901, statements made by the candidate embarrassed the church. As a result a Declaration of Principles was published disavowing the concept of "kingdom" by the church as anything other than a millennial eventuality. See footnote 151, infra. The necessity arose because of the text of Parley P. Pratt's *Key to Theology*, which states on pages 68-69 that the church's priesthood held "the right to give laws and commandments to individuals, churches, rulers, nations, and the world; to appoint, ordain and establish constitutions and kingdoms: to appoint kings, presidents, governors or judges." Parley P. Pratt, *Key to Theology*, (George Q. Cannon & Sons, Salt Lake City, 1891, fifth edition).

[329]   His book, *Joseph Smith: Rough Stone Rolling*, (Knopf, New York, 2005), is not a traditional apology, and was sold in LDS Church owned Deseret Bookstores. Some fellow-Mormons took offense at the book's faithlessness. Those reviews can be read at Amazon.com.

blessings in 1960.[330] A direct lineal descendant of his, Rex Lee, was my Law School Dean at Brigham Young's J. Reuben Clark Law School. His son, Michael Lee, is a US Senator from Utah, and another son, Thomas Lee, is currently a Utah Supreme Court justice. The early events of Utah's history are not distant from living citizens. The dead are an integral part of prominent families who remain anxious to defend ancestral honor.[331] It is easy to confuse dispassion with an attack, making any discussion still problematic among Latter-day Saints.

In the recent book coauthored by Polly Aird, Jeff Nichols and Will Bagley, there is an observation in the *Preface* discussing the challenge of dispassionate history:

> An odd defensiveness still characterizes the "faithful" version of Mormon history, which occasionally borders on paranoia: the mildest critical analysis is often condemned as yet another example of the faith's long-sanctified history of persecution. To this day, the religion's protectors paint the motives of those who do not subscribe to their faith-promoting version of history as suspect. Among defenders of the faith, firsthand critical commentaries on Mormon theocracy can be dismissed as prejudicial and thus ignored. This is true even if these sources describe the reality of life in Utah Territory much more accurately than the fairy-tale

---

[330] John D. Lee died claiming he was a "scapegoat" and not the one primarily responsible for the killings. He was a member of the Council of Fifty, and its scribe for part of his life. His final *Confessions* included the declaration: "I am a true believer in the gospel of Jesus Christ, I do not believe everything that is now being taught and practiced by Brigham Young. I do not care who hears it. It is my last word—it is so. I believe he is leading the people astray, downward to destruction. But I believe in the gospel that was taught in its purity by Joseph Smith, in former days. I have my reasons for it." *Mormonism Unveiled, Or Life & Confessions of John D. Lee*, (Fierra Blanca Publications, Albuquerque, New Mexico, 2001), 394.

[331] Professor Thomas G. Alexander, who responded to the excerpt from this paper at the 2012 Sunstone Symposium mentioned his own ancestral connection to Kirtland and Nauvoo.

history so tediously defended in Apostle Orson F. Whitney's *History of Utah* and more competently argued in B.H. Robert's official chronicles. At times it seems that any scholar not thumping a tub for the restored Gospel is untrustworthy and relegated to an enemies' list dating all the way back to the 1830's.[332]

We will never understand the full implications of Brigham Young's kingship unless we are also willing to recognize the contours and trends of his administration. If we accept his words, he believed sincerely in his kingship. If we accept his rhetoric, he intended to either frighten his wayward subjects to repent or flee. Failing repentance or removal from the kingdom, he fully expected some to be killed. The question is left to each of us to decide how much or how little of what Brigham Young said we will take at face value.

In the Reformation, "[s]uccess could also be measured by the plans of a certain class of people to leave Utah in the spring. Brigham Young summarized these indications of successful reformation in January 1857: 'the reformation still continues …Meetings are frequent and well attended. You may believe that it makes the 'Sinner in Zion afraid, and fearfulness seize the hypocrite, and we trust it will be too warm for such characters to remain in our midst.'"[333]

The New York Times reported in August:

We have another arrival from Mormondom. An emigrant train, containing a large number of women and children – one hundred persons in all—has just reached this city [Lawrence, Kansas] …The members of this company are,

---

[332] *Playing with Shadows: Voices of Dissent in the Mormon West*, (Arthur H. Clark, Norman, Oklahoma, 2011) 13.

[333] Parshall, 68, (internal quotation marks corrected).

or rather were, professors of the Mormon faith, but they have fled from the holy land, partly to escape from the relentless tyranny of the Brigham Young oligarchy, and partly to improve their pecuniary affairs. When they left, there was great dissatisfaction among the Saints, and about a thousand persons abandoned Utah at the same time. Several trains departed for the States, and nearly four hundred started for Oregon. It was with difficulty that they escaped, and many threats were made that violence would be committed upon them if they attempted to leave the country. The large number of those who left is believed to have been their protection.[334]

The exodus from Utah was deliberately provoked. President Young admonished them to leave if they wouldn't subordinate themselves completely to God's kingdom. The Reformation included a twenty-seven question interrogation put to all the saints by inquisitorial Home Missionaries. These questions asked about issues such as "betraying your brothers or sisters," committing adultery or shedding innocent blood.[335] These three sins were grounds for blood atonement. The questions were designed to bring into the homes of every resident of the kingdom the reality that their unfaithfulness may not be tolerated by the kingdom.

In his August 17, 1856 address he proclaimed just how complete surrender must be: Either surrender and follow the kingdom

---

[334] *New York Times*, August 5, 1857; cited in footnote 8, page 68 of Parshall.

[335] The first four questions were: "Have you committed murder, by shedding innocent blood, or consenting thereto? Have you betrayed your brethren or sisters in anything? Have you committed adultery, by having any connection with a woman that was not your wife or a man that was not your husband? Have you taken and made use of property not your own, without the consent of the owner?" For a complete list see Paul H. Peterson, *The Mormon Reformation of 1856-1857: The Rhetoric and the Reality*, Journal of Mormon History, Vol. 15, 1989, 59, 70.

and its leader, or leave it.[336] But he warns if you leave, you will ultimately be destroyed by God; completely annihilated:

> I do not wish you to think that I chastise good men and good women; chastisements do not belong to them, but we have some unruly people here, those who know the law of God, but will not abide it. They have to be talked to; and we have to keep talking to them, and talking to them, until by and by they will forsake their evils, and turn round and become good people, or take up their line of march and leave us...
>
> The principles of eternity and eternal exaltation are of no use to us, unless they are brought down to our capacities so that we practice them in our lives. We must learn the principles of government, must learn ourselves, the eternal government of our God, the interest that the Father has here on the earth and the interest that we have; then we will place our interest with the interest of our Father and God, and will have no self-interest, no interest only in His kingdom that is set up on the earth; then we will begin and apply these principles in our lives ...
>
> The moment a person decides to leave this people, he is cut off from every object that is durable for time and eternity, and I have told you the reason why. Everything that is opposed to God and His Son Jesus Christ, to the celestial kingdom and to celestial laws, those celestial laws and beings will hold warfare with, until every particle of the opposite is turned back to its native element, though it should take millions and millions of ages to accomplish it. Christ

---

[336] By June 7, 1857 President Young commented on the success of this intimidation program: "The spirit of reformation has taken hold on the people; it has kindled the fire of the Almighty in Mount Zion to burn out many of the ungodly that could not stand it, and they have fled...I hope this fire will continue to burn among this people until those poor, miserable curses-those poor, miserable gentlemen, shall all leave us, I pray that the fire of God may burn them out. I pray for this continually." *Complete Discourses*, Vol. 3, 1274-75.

will never cease the warfare, until he destroys death and him that hath the power of it. Every possession and object of affection will be taken from those who forsake the truth, and their identity will eventually cease.[337]

Beginning in mid-November 1856, and continuing through April 1857, President Young forbade the entire church from administering and receiving the sacrament.[338] In October and November, the Willie and Martin Handcart disaster happened. On December 1, 1856 President Young's fellow counselor, and Mormon Reformation advocate Jedediah Grant died prematurely at age 40. The second terrible winter not only claimed livestock, but several Salt Lake homes collapsed under the weight of the snow. The roof of the Bowery on the temple block where church conferences were held also gave way. Instead of questioning the propriety of his "kingship," these signs instead reconfirmed to Brigham Young the need for rigor within his kingdom. President Young added a new threat: "frequently giv[ing] warning that if the people did not reform, they would be left without their leaders and lose the higher (Melchizedek) priesthood."[339] To emphasize the threat, Brigham Young went into hiding for over a month.[340]

Daniel H. Wells replaced Jedediah Grant in the First Presidency of the church. Wells was also the Lieutenant General leader of the

---

[337] *Complete Discourses*, Vol. 2, 1149-55, August 17, 1856.

[338] Parshall, 67-68; Paul H. Peterson, 77.

[339] Paul H. Peterson, 74, also: "The members were warned that the higher priesthood would depart into the wilderness among either the Lamanites or the Ten Tribes, and the Saints would be left with the Aaronic (lower) Priesthood and the law of carnal commandments." *Id.*, citing *Richard Ballantyne Journal*, December 28, 2856, MS, Church Archives; *Wilford Woodruff Journal*, December 28, 1856; *William Gibson Journal*, December 8, 1856; *Salt Lake City Fifth Ward Teachers Meetings Minutes*, MS, Church Archives, December 9, 1856.

[340] Paul H. Peterson, 76.

Nauvoo Legion. Like Grant before him, his fidelity was to Brigham Young and the kingdom, not the United States. On February 8, 1857, President Young instructed his kingdom:

> I could refer you to plenty of instances where men have been righteously slain, in order to atone for their sins. I have seen scores and hundreds of people for whom there would have been a chance (in the last resurrection there will be) if their lives had been taken and their blood spilled on the ground as a smoking incense to the Almighty, but who are now angels to the devil, until our elder brother Jesus Christ raises them up —conquers death, hell and the grave. I have known a great many men who have left this Church for whom there is no chance whatever for exaltation, but if their blood had been spilled, it would have been better for them… If you have sinned a sin requiring the shedding of blood, except the sin unto death, would not be satisfied nor rest until your blood should be spilled, that you might gain that salvation you desire. That is the way to love mankind.[341]

Two days prior to this talk, as he emerged from hiding, Governor Young issued letters on February 6, 1857 instructing violence be used to punish several targeted individuals known to have violated the law. One letter was addressed to three recipients, including stake president Isaac C. Haight[342] at Cedar City. The letter stated,

> Be on the look out now, & have a few trusty men ready in the case of need to pursue, retake & punish. We do not suppose there would be any prosecutions for false imprisonment, or tale bearers for witnesses… Make no noise of

---

[341] *Complete Discourses*, Vol. 3, 1229, February 8, 1857.

[342] Isaac C. Haight's area included Mountain Meadows, and he supervised John D. Lee.

this matter, & keep this letter safe. We write for your eye alone, & to men that can be trusted.[343]

The letter resulted in the Santa Clara Ambush, which is the topic of Parshall's article in *The Utah Historical Quarterly*, cited earlier. News of the ambush found its way into newspapers throughout the United States. Parshall explains:

> The Santa Clara ambush was not what Brigham Young intended, in that it was not two backsliding felons who were attacked in the dark. But the ambush was the result of events he set in motion. He directed subordinates to take extra-legal action under specified conditions, knowing that innocents might suffer with the guilty because no "tale bearers" were to be spared. If he did not intend Dame and Haight to read his instructions as they have been interpreted here, that reading is justified by the indirect phrasing of his letters. If residents of southern Utah went beyond the mark in implementing his instructions, no effective chastisements occurred. All of the men to whom letters were sent retained their church, civil and military positions as though nothing untoward happened.

> But something had happened, with repercussions beyond the injuries and losses to Tobin and his companions. News of the attack spread quickly through the nation, heightening tensions on the eve of the Utah War. When the wounded victims were carried to San Bernadino, rumors flared that endangered the lives of Mormons living there. Lack of accountability following the Santa Clara ambush did nothing to allay a local impression that violence was a suitable response to perceived threat, an impression, which seemingly played a role at Mountain Meadows later that year. Most chilling to contemplate, survival of the Santa

---

[343] See Parshall, 74, quoting letter of February 6, 1857 from the Brigham Young Collection of letters in the Archives of The Church of Jesus Christ of Latter-day Saints.

Clara victims and their public exposure of the attack may have strengthened a determination at Mountain Meadows to spare no competent witness.[344]

The Santa Clara ambush may have included unintended victims. The action may have been well beyond the intent of Brigham Young when he wrote the instructions. However, Parshall's explanation above is inadequate. If Brigham Young wrote the letter as a king, as head of both church and state, then the process was not "extra-legal" at all. It was a sovereign's right to issue the order. He was imposing order, as was the king's right to do.[345]

As 1857 continued, the king's ire spread from "reigning pitchforks"[346] from the podium, to the fruit of his rhetoric that cost some their lives. After Santa Clara, the violence spread. As it spread, neither the church nor the state over which Brigham Young presided displayed any inclination to hold a single person accountable for the deaths. Beyond that, there was no curiosity to find out the truth, or identify those involved. Parshall describes the events of that turbulent year:

> Failure to hold anyone responsible for the Santa Clara ambush foreshadowed the silence to follow the Potter-Parish murders in Springville the next month, the massacre at Mountain Meadows in September, the October bludgeoning death of Richard Yates in Echo Canyon, the murders of the Aiken party near Nephi in November — a catalog of

---

[344] Parshall, 84-85.

[345] "We know that the world is angry at us, and that we cannot help. We mean to pursue our course, build up the kingdom of God on earth, and establish Zion. We have also got to assist in rebuilding Jerusalem[.]" *Complete Discourses*, Vol. 3, 1277, June 7, 1857.

[346] This was the phrase used in his March 2, 1856 talk; see footnote 74, supra.

bloodshed without accountability in the surreal year of 1857.[347]

The events were too much. The United States was buzzing with alarm. The Utah Territorial Legislature issued a proclamation claiming the Territory's law was superior to Federal Law. New First Presidency member and commander of the Nauvoo Legion, Daniel Wells, issued General Order 1 at the beginning of April. This order was "notifying Nauvoo Legion members that they now belonged to the armed forces of God's Kingdom."[348] "President Buchanan in late May decided to unseat [Brigham Young] as governor and ordered the US Army to escort his successor to Great Salt Lake to restore federal authority in Utah."[349] Given Brigham Young's widely reported refusal to surrender the Governorship unless "God Almighty" would tell him to submit, President Buchanan concluded the US Army was necessary to install a new Governor. This has been called The Utah War, or The Mormon Rebellion.

The Utah War has been characterized as a "bloodless" event. When it concluded in 1858, the *New York Herald* observed it "may thus be summarily historized:—killed, none; wounded, none, fooled, everybody."[350] Recent scholarship has revisited the war, and at least one scholar changed his view from being "bloodless" to being quite bloody. His revised view is now:

Overlooked or intentionally excluded from these views is the Mountain Meadows Massacre as a wartime engagement on September 11, 1857. It was an atrocity in which a de-

---

[347] Parshall, 84-85.

[348] David L. Bigler and Will Bagley, *The Mormon Rebellion: American's First Civil War, 1857-1858*, (University of Oklahoma, Norman, 2011), 114.

[349] *Id.*, 132.

[350] *New York Herald*, July 19, 1858.

tachment of the Utah territorial militia (Nauvoo Legion) supported by Indian auxiliaries executed about 120 disarmed men, women and children, the largest organized mass murder of white civilians in American history until the 1995 Oklahoma City bombing.[351]

That author goes on to put the entire sweep of violence in Brigham Young's kingdom in 1857 into the wartime context. When that is done, he concludes the Utah War rivaled "Bleeding Kansas" in fatalities.[352]

The violence of Mormons in that aberrational year has been difficult to justify. It is a milestone departure from all prior Mormon conduct. Mormons transitioned from victims to murderers. One recent attempt explains it this way:

> Scholars who have investigated violence in many cultures provide other insights based on group psychology. Episodes of violence often begin when one people classify another as "the other," stripping them of any humanity and mentally transforming them into enemies. Once this process of devaluing and demonizing occurs, stereotypes take over, rumors circulate, and pressure builds to conform to group action against the perceived threat. Those classified as the enemy are often seen as the transgressors, even as steps are being taken against them. When these tinderbox conditions exist, a single incident, small or ordinary in usual circumstances, may spark great violence ending in atrocity.

> The literature suggests other elements are often present when "good people" do terrible things. Usually there is an atmosphere of authority and obedience, which allows errant leaders to trump the moral instincts of their followers.

---

[351] William P. MacKinnon, *Lonely Bones: Leadership and Utah War Violence*, Journal of Mormon History, Vol. 33, No. 1, 2007, 124.

[352] Id., 124-25.

Atrocities also occur when followers do not have clear messages about what is expected of them—when their culture
or message from headquarters leave local leaders wonder-
ing what they should do. Poverty increases the likelihood of
problems by raising concerns about survival. The conditions for mass killing—demonizing, authority, obedience,
peer pressure, ambiguity, fear, and deprivation—all were
present in southern Utah in 1857.[353]

Of these conditions, Brigham Young's leadership supplied the
demonizing, authority, obedience, peer pressure, ambiguity and fear.
His purpose was to establish this very environment. Brigham
Young's own son would characterize the Reformation as "a reign of
terror."[354] One woman who lived through that time reflected: "it
was a fearful ordeal, and fear is a slavish passion and is not begotten
by the Spirit of God!"[355]

This was Brigham Young's purpose and he said he understood
exactly how to govern to accomplish what was needed. He explained how few men were qualified, as he was, to lead people to
accomplish what a leader wanted:

There are but few men who know how to govern in temporal
things, fewer still who know how to control the feelings of the people, how to guide the power of any kingdom that was ever organized on the earth. Nations and kingdoms of this world rise up and
flourish only for a season. What is the difficulty? They contain the
seeds of their own destruction, sown therein by the framers of human governments; those combustive elements are organized in their

---

353   Walker, Turley, Leonard, Preface xiv.

354   *Brigham Young Jr. Diary*, December 15, 1862.

355   *Hannah Tapfield King Diary*, October 8, 1856, cited in Bigler & Bagley, 98, and footnote 13. Her diary is one of the more important sources for information during this
period.

constitution from the first…Why are they thus led to sow the seeds of their own destruction? Because the kingdoms of this world are not designed to stand. When men are placed at the head of government who are not actually controlled by the power of God by the Holy Ghost they can lay plans, they can frame constitutions, they can form governments and laws that have not the seeds of death within them, and no other men can do it.[356]

If we take him at his word, then the deathly harvest of 1857 was what he hoped to accomplish. Often overlooked by all writers is the claim that he knew exactly what he was doing, and was controlled by the power of God through the Holy Ghost, therefore perfectly capable of achieving what he intended through his subjects.

There is another rhetorical milestone immediately prior to the tragedy of the Mountain Meadows Massacre. In August 1857, Governor Young knew the Army had been dispatched to install a new Governor. He learned on the 11th that the Army had arrived 118 miles below Laramie.[357] On the 16th he gave a talk about the Army, his intent to fight them, and the direful results the nation should expect if they persisted in moving forward into combat with the kingdom. Only 26 days prior to the Mountain Meadows Massacre, Governor Young warned the United States:

> Now if the United States send an army here and commences war on us, their travel across this country must stop; their train cannot cross. To accomplish this I need only say to them for the Indians will use them up; and they

---

[356] *Complete Discourses*, Vol. 2, 1233, March 8, 1857.

[357] "On Friday evening, the 11th inst. two of the brethren who accompanied brothers Samuel W. Richards and George Snider from Deer Creek to 118 miles below Laramie, came in, and reported that soldiers and a heavy freight train were there encamped opposite to them and on the south side of the Platte." *Complete Discourses*, Vol. 3, 1329-30; September 6, 1857.

will do it...I warn them and fore warn the United States, that if they commence war upon us, they need not expect me to hold the Indians while they shoot them...

Had it not been for the "Mormons" in these mountains, nineteen out of twenty of this seasons emigration would have been cut off by the Indians. Had it not for our settlements here, overland emigration would have been stopped years ago, and yet they turn around and condemn me and this people for conniving with the Indians. This people have always done good to the travelers; they have kept the Indians from injuring them and have done all in their power to save the lives of men, women and children, but all this will cease to be, if our enemies commence war upon us.[358]

Twenty-six days later a Mormon led attack killed over one-hundred twenty men, women and children. The slaughter was staged to look Indian caused,[359] and reported as an Indian attack;[360] as if the event was quick proof of the seriousness of the Governor's warning. The proximity of the talk and the attack appeared to

---

[358] *Id.*, Vol. 3, 1321, August 16, 1857.

[359] Men, women and children were all killed. Unlike Indians, white attacks normally would not include women and children as victims. The bodies were stripped and all belongings and livestock were all stolen. These were typical of Indian attacks, and staged here to conceal Mormon involvement.

[360] "In the years following the mass killing, the white participants persisted in blaming the tragedy primarily on the Paiutes. Even [Nephi] Johnson, who saw most of what happened from his position on the hill, at times joined in the finger-pointing. But during a conversation with a senior Mormon leader from Salt Lake City in 1895, Johnson said that 'white men did most of the killing.'" (Ronald W. Walker, Richard E. Turley, Glen M. Leonard, *Massacre at Mountain Meadows*, (Oxford University, 2008), 204, citations omitted.) *Wilford Woodruff's Journal* reported on May 25, 1861: "We visited the Mountain Meadow Monument put up at the burial place of 120 persons killed by Indians in 1857. The pile of stone was about 12 feet high, but beginning to tumble down. A wooden Cross was placed on top with the following words: Vengeance is mine and I will repay, saith the Lord. President Young said it should be: Vengeance is mine and I have taken a little." (Vol. 5, 577.)

be swift vindication, but did not deter the Army's progress or the United States' determination to remove Governor Young.

As the Army approached, Governor Young repeatedly warned them against coming. Not only would Indian uprisings afflict the United States,[361] but God would also come out of His hiding place and fight for the kingdom.[362] He predicted a spectacular defeat, with the unseen "soldiers of the Lord" defending the kingdom.[363] The

---

[361] A month before Mountain Meadows Massacre, he prayed: "We also pray the [sic] our Father to turn the hearts of the Lamanites even the sons of Jacob unto us that they may do thy will & be as a wall of defense around about us." *Complete Discourses*, Vol. 3, 1315, August 9, 1857. Two days after the Massacre he declared again: "Again if they Commence the war I shall not hold the Indians Still by the fist any longer for white men to shoot at them but I shall let them go ahead & do as they please and I shall Carry the war into their own land and they will want to let out the Job before they get half through." *Id.*, 1342, September 13, 1857. Seven months later he reiterated: "President B Young said If the US Troops make a war of extermination against this People they will have all the Indians on this Continent to Fight for they are of Israel and the Course which the army are now taking towards them will have a tendency to cause the Indians to make war upon them." *Id.*, 1426, April 15, 1858.

[362] "You need have no fear but the fear to offend God. If you have any trembling in your hearts, or timid feelings with regard to our present situation, let me tell you one thing, which is as true as that the sun now shines, that whatever transpires with us, with our enemies, with the world here or there, will still more promote the kingdom of God on earth, and bring to a final end the kingdoms of this world...The world are determined to destroy the kingdom of God upon the earth; they wish to obliterate it. The kingdoms of darkness are determined to destroy this kingdom. In their feelings they are fighting against you and me, and do not know that they are contending against Jehovah. They have not the least idea of that, but think they are contending against the 'Mormons.' They are not contending against you and me—they are contending against the God of heaven." *Complete Discourses*, Vol. 3, 1289-90, June 28, 1857. "Be faithful, and God will not only fight for us, but will also lead us to victory. What has been said today is true." *Id.*, 1344, September 20, 1857.

[363] "Yes; there are ten to one for us more than those against us; but the difficulty is that all have not eyes to see. The soldiers of the Lord are in the mountains, in the canyons, upon the plains, on the hills, along the mighty streams, and by the rivulets. Thousands and thousands more are for us than those who are against us, and you need not have any fears. They may be permitted to kill our bodies, but that is yet to be determined. They try to fire a pistol; the cap snaps, and they are in the lurch; for some would have dagger into them before they would know it. Or, if they tried to shoot with a rifle, perhaps the person aimed at would be standing a little one side of the range of the bullet." *Complete Discourses*, Vol. 3, 1302, July 19, 1857. This prediction of misaimed fire is akin to the Book of Mormon account of Samuel the Lamanite, who could not be hit with stones or arrows aimed at him. See Helaman 16: 2-3, 6.

threatened war and the prospects of the kingdom defeating the coming Army pleased Governor Young. He proclaimed:

> I do not know that I have ever felt better in my life, more satisfied, more rejoicing in my heart, or had more of the testimony and witness of the Spirit within, than when I have said, You Latter day Saints may be driven to move, if you will take your own part, and "I the Lord your God am with you, and I will help you and I will fight your battles." It is rather a bold statement; it is rather a bold step for a handful of men here in the mountains to think that they can cope with the extensive government, the government of the United States, the powerful kingdoms of darkness. Upon natural principles we cannot, but we can fight them in the name of, God Almighty, and with his aid we can keep them off from us.[364]

This pleasure was in part because of his belief war prevented apostasy.[365] He warned the United States not to come because they risked utter defeat.[366] The whole world was watching this conflict, making God's Kingdom renown.[367] The outcome of this conflict

---

[364] *Collected Discourses*, Vol. 3, 1317, August 16, 1857.

[365] "I was not afraid of men's apostatizing when war and trouble are on hand, for then they will stick together. It is in calm weather, when the old ship of Zion is sailing with a gentle breeze, and when all is quiet on deck, that some of the brethren want to go out in the whaling-boats to have a scrape and a swim; and some get drowned, others drift away, and others again get back to the ship." *Id.*, 1401, January 17, 1858.

[366] "But I warn and fore warn our enemies to let this people alone. The Elders of Israel are almighty, and it will soon be said, 'let us not go up to Zion, for the inhabitants of Zion are terrible.'" *Id.*, 1320.

[367] "There has been a great deal said in the lower world about this little handful of people; for you terrify the whole world! Not alone in the United States, but in England, in France, in Italy, in Germany, and in every State upon the eastern continent, the people are looking to see the result of the present movements of our Government towards this people." *Id.*, 1326, August 30, 1857.

was certain.[368] Brigham Young asked, "Cannot this kingdom be overthrown? No. They might as well try to obliterate the sun."[369] It was not the kingdom Brigham Young led that was vulnerable to destruction, but the United States was at peril and about to be destroyed by God.[370] He said "millions" would die in the conflict, and he expected to live to see his kingdom govern throughout the continent.[371] The destruction of the US Army was, according to Governor Young, part of God's design to acquire a respected name and a fearful character again in this world.[372] Terrorized European nations would soon remove their hats in reverence when Mormons

---

[368] "While we have been learning how to sustain the kingdom of God upon the earth, the Devil and his pupils have been learning how to sustain the kingdom of darkness. From the very nature of the two kingdoms upon one planet, the crisis must come where there will be a literal open warfare, just as much as there is now a warfare within us against evil; …[T]he spirits of darkness will have to give way to the kingdom of God, and that 'Mormonism' will triumph, and that no power can hinder it." *Id.*, 1348-49, October 7, 1957.

[369] *Id.*

[370] "President B. Young in his Sermon declared that the thread was cut between us and the U.S. and that the Almighty recognized us as a free and independent people and that no officer appointed by government sent to should come and rule us from this time forth." *Id.*, 1332, September 6, 1857. "I do not want to fight the United States but if they drive us to it we shall do the best we can & I will tell you as God lives that we shall Come off Conqueror for we trust in God. For God has set up his kingdom on the Earth & it will never fall but it will stand. We shall do all we can not to fight but if they drive us to it God will overthrow them. *Id*, September 12, 1857.

[371] "God and the Saints being my helper I will make millions of them bite the dust before I go through the vale. These are my private feelings. If they will persist in trying to take away my life, they have got a job on hand if the Lord continues to be on my side, and I think he will if I do not forsake him and his commandments…I mean to live until their names are forgotten from the earth, until Zion is established on this continent, and the law of Zion is the law of the land, and the people are governed by the eternal priesthood." *Id.*, 1394, 1395, January 16, 1858.

[372] "The Lord Almighty wants a name and a character; and he will show our enemies that he is God, and that he has set to his hand again to gather Israel, and to try our faith and integrity. And he is saying, 'Now, you, my children, dare you take a step to promote righteousness, in direct and open opposition to the popular feelings of all the wicked in your Government? If you do, I will fight your battles.'" *Id.*, 1341, September 13, 1857. "The great God has set this hand to roll forth his purposes, and the hand that opposes it shall be palsied. The power of God shall be felt among the nations that reject the truth." *Id.*, 1362, October 31, 1857.

passed through.[373] Some of his rhetoric is reminiscent of Sidney Rigdon's excesses during the succession debates in Nauvoo, fourteen years earlier.[374]

As King Brigham preached to the Utah Legislature during the winter of 1857, the US Army was quartered down for winter still hundreds of hard miles away. He believed his kingdom would not only win this conflict, but the triumph would lead to control over all nations by God's kingdom—over which Brigham Young would preside:

> The Lord should reign and rule over us in all our business transactions The Kingdom of God is one thing, and the Church of Jesus Christ of Latter Day Saints is another, yet it is one, and when the Kingdom of God is set up upon the earth it will be a temporal Kingdom, and that is the King-

---

[373] "[T]he news will go that there a people in the mountains called Mormons, and that they are in the fastness of the rocky mountains, and the United States can do nothing with them, and the time will soon be that their name and sound, and the pride of the people will be, 'I am from Utah,' and I am a Latter day saint, and this will strike terror to the Christian and to the heathen world, and that time is close at hand. And let me say while upon this subject that if there is a much performed in ten years to come, as has been in ten years past that time will not pass till our government and the Governments of Europe will take off their hats, and make a bow. When that time comes lean then say to a State, to England, to France, to the German States, or any other kingdom on the earth 'Let our Elders in there, or we will attend to your case; you bar your gates against our Elders, and I am after you; let them go in peace and preach the gospel to the poor.'" *Id.*, 1385, December 25, 1857.

[374] Sidney Rigdon's propensity for elevated rhetoric, on display in August, 1844, was one of the reasons the Saints voted against his claim to be the church's guardian. "Declaring that the Lord's ways were not their ways, he veered into his favorite topic, the prophecies of Armageddon. The time was near at hand, he warned, when the Saints 'would see one hundred tons of metal per second thrown at the enemies of God,' and blood would flow as deep as the 'horses' bridles.' With his usual extravagance he trumpeted: 'I am going to fight a real bloody battle with sword and with gun ...I will fight the battles of the Lord. I will also cross the Atlantic, encounter the queen's forces, and overcome them—plant the American standard on English ground, and then march to the palace of her majesty, and demand a portion of her riches and dominions, which if she refuse, I will take the little madam by the nose and lead her out, and she shall have no power to help herself. If I do not do this, the Lord never spake by mortal.'" Richard S. VanWagoner, *Sidney Rigdon: A Portrait of Religious Excess*, (Signature Books, Salt Lake City, 1994), 337, footnotes omitted.

dom Jesus referred to, and which his saints would fight for. The Kingdom of God is a temporal Kingdom and the Church of Jesus Christ is His Church and Kingdom. The Kingdom of God will enact laws that will govern and control all people whether Saint or sinner, whether they worship God, the Sun, Moon or Stars. The Law that will issue forth, from Zion will control the nations of the Earth, and give to each one his rights in the free exercise and enjoyment of his[.] ...Here is the Kingdom of God in embryo, which will enact laws for the Government of all people, nations, kindreds and tongues upon the face of the whole earth, and in our deliberations our eyes should be single to this point, that this doctrine has been preached and acted upon, and the Kingdom of God was organized in the days of Joseph [Smith], and was called the council of Fifty, and that was the commencement for to issue forth laws for the nations of the earth.[375]

As God's earthly king, established through the Council of Fifty, Governor Young remained defiant of federal authority. He an-

---

[375] *Id.*, 1381, December 15, 1857.

swered to a higher authority.[376] But no higher authority rallied the Indians, nor came out from His hiding place to destroy the Army, nor caused unseen soldiers to slay US forces. Instead, the Army came and Brigham Young negotiated an end to his earthly rule over the Utah Territory. He served a total of seven years, although appointed only for four. The act allowed him to continue "until his successor shall be appointed and qualified, unless sooner removed by the President of the United States." Governor Cumming peacefully assumed office in April of 1858, and was introduced by Brigham Young to a congregation of Saints as "my friend Gov. Cummings" on April 25, 1858.[377] After all the preliminary excitement lasting for two years prior to his arrival, the transition was cordial.

---

[376]   In mid-winter, 1858, while US troops waited for Spring to resume their march to Utah, Brigham Young explained his understanding of God's great plan. In the beginning of man, the original revelation from God to Adam "was of a temporal nature. Most of the revelations he received pertained to his life here. That was also the case in the revelations to Noah. We have but very few of the instructions the Lord gave to Enoch concerning his city; but, doubtless, most of the revelations he received pertained to a temporal nature and condition. And certainly the revelation Noah received, so far as in our possession, almost exclusively pertained to this life. The same principle was carried out in the days of Moses, and in the days of his fathers, Abraham, Isaac, and Jacob. We may say that eight or nine-tenths of the doctrines and principles set forth in the revelations given to those men were of a temporal nature." He went on to contrast that with Christ: "The greatest recorded digression from that course was when the Saviour came. He repeatedly alluded to a spiritual kingdom, in his sayings to his brethren. The people had become so corrupt that it was all useless to then endeavour to establish a literal kingdom of God on the earth…[T]he Saviour had not opportunity to more than drop a hint, as it were, about a temporal kingdom…The first revelations given to Joseph were of a temporal character, pertaining to a literal kingdom on the earth." He went on to assert that the missionary work of the church was so converts' "eyes may be open to see that the Lord is commencing a literal kingdom upon the earth." The conflict with the US was to make that kingdom independent. "[T]he Lord in his providence led the people into these mountains to separate them from the Gentile world, in order that he might establish his kingdom—his laws, and commence his Zion in the mountains, where his people could have but little connection with the world. They were taught that when they first came here; and now the prospect is very fair for separating us from the rest of the world, and most of the people can see it." *Id.*, 1398-99, January 17, 1858.

[377]   *Id.*, 1427.

A Telestial Kingship

Mormonism may have ended at the death of Joseph Smith if not for Brigham Young's leadership. Because he acted decisively, The Church of Jesus Christ of Latter-day Saints remains an organized body of believers, perpetuating the structure established through Joseph. Mormonism was preserved in structure, but altered in content with Brigham Young at the helm. History has acknowledged his great contribution in preserving the faith, but it has not yet adequately acknowledged how greatly he changed the content and practice of Mormonism.

Many of the most provocative statements of Governor Young and violent acts by Mormons were reported in the national press at the time. As mentioned before, the resulting public impression was so unfavorable, the President was compelled to send the US Army to intervene. This extraordinary action was popularly approved because of the belief Brigham Young had established a despotic and rebellious monarchy in the Rocky Mountains, and nothing short of intervention by an armed force could end it.

Almost every religion has some doctrine(s) beyond man's capacity to implement. Until Saint Francis accomplished it, Catholicism doubted man's capacity to live the Sermon on the Mount for over a thousand years. Few have repeated his achievement. Nevertheless, the ideal remains firmly a part of Catholicism.

All Mormon men may be called to rise up by heaven's invitation and become something more, something far greater in Mormonism's priestly service, but few are ever chosen by heaven to do so. This is because it is so easy to stray from the virtues of meekness, humility and gentleness to pursue earthly ambition, control or dominion. Mormon scripture laments this near-universal propensity to fail.[378]

Kingship is perhaps both the greatest ideal and worst tempta-tion in Mormon Theology. Brigham Young's belief in his status as a king is strengthened when the comments of other church authori-ties are considered. This paper confined the topic to Brigham Young's own comments, and therefore, none of those others are included. The difficulty of acting as a king is on public display in the Governorship of Brigham Young.[379] His is a cautionary tale for us about the greatest challenge faced by faithful Mormons who hope to be sons of God and joint-heirs with His Son.[380]

John Locke wrote in his *Second Treatise of Civil Government* that "all princes and rulers of independent governments all throughout the world, are in a state of nature[.]"[381] Brigham Young viewed his status as God's earthly head of an independent kingdom, and conformed conduct to that view. Therefore, as John Locke would expect, his behavior was like man "in a state of nature" where he had the right to "restrain, or where it is necessary, destroy things noxious to [him]."[382] Locke's description is apt.

---

[378]   D&C 121: 34-42.

[379]   Governor Young believed fervently in his Divine appointment because he believed fervently in Joseph Smith. He attributed his behavior to his sincere desire to accomplish the purposes which Joseph originally held: "We could not stay in the States, and if we had gone to Texas, where Lyman White [sic] went, before this day the Saints would have been driven from there. Such would have been the case if we had gone to any other place but in the midst of these Mountains. There is the place when Joseph said we could build up the kingdom of God, and all hell could not remove it. He tried to get us here, and talked of it year after in our private counsels. A great many have wondered how I came here. Joseph talked about it, when he had his brethren about him, for years, and we knew all about it." *Complete Discourses*, Vol. 3, 1285-86, June 21, 1857.

[380]   See 1 John 3: 2; Romans 8: 17.

[381]   Locke, Chapter 2, Section 14.

[382]   *Id.*, Section 8.

Before Governor Young surrendered public office, the President of the United States granted a complete pardon to the Governor and all those who, under his direction, engaged in the Utah War.[383] The pardon given by President Buchanan was the most sweeping granted by a US President at the time and ended both a war and Brigham Young's direct control of the state.

If, during Brigham Young's lifetime, America viewed Mormonism as one of the "twin relics of barbarism," as the Republican Platform Abraham Lincoln ran on described it, subsequent events domesticated Mormonism. Mormonism went from being a Great Basin Monarchy to an uber-American, flag-waving, rock-solid red-state on the most conservative side of the ledger at present. Both the state and church Brigham Young led have become 'house-broken' to

---

[383] Brigham Young said he was mystified by the pardon: "I thank President Buchanan for forgiving me, but I really cannot tell what I have done. I know one thing, and that is that the people called Mormons are a loyal and law abiding people and have ever been. Neither President Buchanan nor anyone else can contradict that statement." *Complete Discourses*, Vol. 3, 1439, June 12, 1858.

Americanism.[384] This year's Presidential election reflects the long road Governor Young's people have travelled.[385]

Explaining the violence in Utah during the tenure of Governor Young, one writer says this: "the point here is not to claim that no vigilante crimes by angry Mormons protecting their interests ever occurred in territorial Utah. The point is that over-attention to such activities obscures the fact that they were very rare compared to elsewhere in the West, where no concerted effort to undermine a popularly supported government was going on as in Utah."[386] This measure concedes too much. It presumes to compare God's kingdom to how others in this world behave; in Mormon vocabulary, the standard is Telestial.

---

[384] "Church leaders also reinterpreted the doctrine of the Kingdom of God to push its earthy application into the millennium. Instead of arguing, as church leaders like Parley P. Pratt in the nineteenth century had, that the priesthood-directed Kingdom of God was the only legitimate government on earth, in December 1901 the First Presidency stated that though the church might instruct in temporal as well as spiritual matters, it 'does not infringe upon the liberty of the individual or encroach upon the domain of the State.'" Thomas G. Alexander, *Mormonism in Transition: A History of the Latter-day Saints, 1890-1930*, (University of Illinois, Urbana, 1986), 289.

[385] During an earlier political campaign involving church leader B.H. Roberts' bid for election to Congress, the First Presidency of the church thought Elder Roberts went too far in stating church ambitions. They issued a Declaration of Truths containing the following retractions of the earlier ambition for a kingdom: "IV. That no church, ecclesiastical body, nor spiritual advisor should encroach upon the political rights of the individual. V. That in a free country no man nor body of men can, with safety to the State, use the name or the power of any religious sect or society to influence or control the elective franchise. VI. That a trust is imposed upon each citizen in a free country to act politically upon his own judgment and absolutely free from control or dictation, ecclesiastical or otherwise." See Michael Harold Paulos, *The Mormon Church on Trial: Transcripts of the Reed Smoot Hearings*, (Signature Books, Salt Lake City, 2008), 219, footnote 8; also the testimony of B.H. Roberts before the Senate beginning on 218-19 where he testifies of the church's abandonment of the ambition for a kingdom in favor of democratic rule.

[386] Eric A. Eliason, *Review of: Forgotten Kingdom: The Mormon Theocracy in the American West, 1847-1896*, FARMS Review of Books 12/1 (2000), 101-102.

When Christ spoke of His kingdom, He declared it was "not of this world."[387] The inspiration for Brigham Young's ambition to be king came from Joseph Smith and the Council of Fifty. But Joseph Smith surrendered his own life, "as a lamb to the slaughter" even when he had the largest militia in Illinois, the Nauvoo Legion, at his command to prevent his arrest.[388] Christ was killed, Joseph Smith was killed, and both claimed an otherworldly kingship. Brigham Young, on the other hand, made it clear he would never submit to similar surrender and self-sacrifice. Referring back to Joseph and Hyrum being killed in Illinois he declared: "I Carried a large Bowie knife with me and I said that any man that laid hands upon my Shoulder and said Mr. Young you are my prisoner I would send that man to hell across lots & I have said that all the time since and I say it now. I have broken no law neither will I be taken by any United States officer to be killed as they have killed Joseph."[389]

The form of kingship demonstrated by Christ and Joseph Smith is approved in the Book of Mormon. In this form the king is servant, and not a master. This form of king is in God's service while kneeling and laboring to serve others, without boasting and without imposing grievous burdens.[390] In other words, the Book of Mormon approves a Celestial kingship, which serves through self-

---

[387]   John 18: 36.

[388]   D&C 135: 4.

[389]   *Complete Discourses*, Vol. 3, 1333; September 12, 1857.

[390]   See Mosiah 2: 14-19.

sacrifice,[391] and meek example as the model of leadership, but utterly rejects control, compulsion and dominion by an earthly king. Hence the sad observation made by Joseph Smith that it is the nature of almost all men as soon as they have a little authority to begin to exercise unrighteous dominion over others.[392]

Mormon apologists do not apply a Celestial standard for the Reformation. Nor do they use the Book of Mormon to measure Governor Young. Consistently, they compare the kingdom's conduct to gentiles elsewhere in the West.[393] By that standard, Governor Young presided over a marginally violent Telestial Kingdom, meriting only an above average grade in the number of killings. In the end, whether you are sympathetic, dispassionate, or critical of this era of Mormon history, all writers Mormon and non-Mormon alike, seem willing to concede it was a Telestial Kingdom over which Governor Young reigned. By that standard he did well enough. However, should Mormons be satisfied? Is it enough that he did not cause more violence? Is Mormonism to be measured against its

---

[391]   Such kings lay down their lives for their friends. (John 15: 13.) In contrast, Brigham Young developed an entirely different approach. Under his administration kings were protected by the subjects who would lay down their lives to protect kings. There were volunteers, like Bishop Warren Snow, who considered it their God-given duty to "stand between" his leaders and all threats. Taking life or sacrificing his own life to preserve church leaders' lives was his "mission." See John A. Peterson, *Warren Stone Snow, A Man In Between: The Biography of a Mormon Defender*, Master's Thesis, BYU, December 1985, 2-7.

[392]   D&C 121: 39: "We have learned by sad experience that it is the nature and disposition of almost all men, as soon as they get a little authority, as they suppose, they will immediately begin to exercise unrighteous dominion."

[393]   Another example of comparing Salt Lake with surrounding areas is in Paul H. Peterson, 73-74: "It would be easy to exaggerate the amount of violence in Utah Territory, however. In an age and a land where violence was commonplace, Salt Lake City and its environs had conspicuously little."

highest ideals, or instead its better-than-average performance?[394] If we use the steep incline in the number of killings beginning in 1857 as a trend, then the fruit of the Mormon Reformation begun the previous year was an ominous harvest. Had the US Government not intervened to remove Governor Young in 1858, the trend suggests something even more dreadful was coming. Perhaps all of us should recognize in Johnson's Army the very thing Brigham Young wanted to hear before he would surrender his Governorship: the voice of God Almighty telling him he no longer needed to be Governor.

President Young lamented that he never was visited by God. He told his followers:

> I have flattered myself, if I am as faithful as I know how to be to my God, and my brethren, and to all my covenants, and faithful in the discharge of my duty, when I have lived to be as old as was Moses when the Lord appeared to him, that perhaps I then may hold communion with the Lord, as did Moses. I am not now in that position, though I know much more than I did twenty, ten, or five years ago. But have I yet lived to the state of perfection that I can commune in person with the Father and the Son at my will and pleasure? No, though I hold myself in readiness that he can wield me at his will and pleasure. If I am faithful until I am eighty years of age, perhaps the Lord will appear to me and personally dictate me in the management of his Church and people. A little over twenty years, and if I am faithful, perhaps I will obtain that favour with my Father and God.[395]

---

[394] Even now Mormons often point to their lower-than-average divorce rate for Temple marriages, rather than the scandal represented by any Temple marriage failing. Tim B. Heaton, *Dealing With Demographics*, at FAIR.org website, explains: "the lifetime divorce rate may be around 25% to 30%. I would guess the temple divorce rate is in that range. It's pretty high, but it's still a lot lower than the national 50% rate." Ideals exceed our grasp, but should be the only aspiration we measure against.

[395] *Complete Discourses*, Vol. 3, 1498, September 1, 1859.

For President Young, in the absence of the Lord appearing "and personally dictat[ing to him] in the management of his Church and people," hearing "the voice of Almighty God" was a matter of common sense. He told the kingdom, after learning that President Buchanan had ordered the Army to go to Utah, how he was able to conduct the kingdom's affairs: "I am not going to interpret dreams; for I don't profess to be such a Prophet as were Joseph Smith and Daniel; but I am a Yankee guesser[.]"[396] From our vantage point, we can question why he did not hear it in the early death of Willard Richards,[397] nor in the drought, grasshopper swarms, crop failures, bitter winters, livestock deaths, buildings collapsing under the weight of unusually heavy winter snows—including the church's Bowery, in the handcart company disasters, premature death of Jedediah Grant,[398] nor in his own life-threatening illness in February 1857. God's voice throughout those difficulties only said to the Yankee guesser that God condemned the subjects of the kingdom for their lack of fidelity to the earthly king's righteous leadership.

The Book of Mormon promises the American continent was to remain a place of liberty.[399] This land is not for kings and kingdoms. The gentile occupants are warned to never establish a king here, or

---

[396] *Id.*, Vol. 3, 1306, July 26, 1857.

[397] Willard Richards died March 11, 1854 at age 49.

[398] Jedediah Grant died December 1, 1856 at age 40.

[399] "Wherefore, this land is consecrated unto him whom he shall bring. And if it so be that they shall serve him according to the commandments which he hath given, it shall be a land of liberty unto them; wherefore, they shall never be brought down into captivity; if so, it shall be because of iniquity; for if iniquity shall abound cursed shall be the land for their sakes, but unto the righteous it shall be blessed forever." (2 Ne. 19: 7.)

they would be cursed.[400] Using the Book of Mormon teachings, the collision between Brigham Young and the United States could be interpreted as a conflict between God's decree against kingship and Governor Young's insistence upon it. In that sense, the arrival of the Army to remove the Governor *was* at last the voice of Almighty God he heard.

Even good men make poor idols. Before reaching a conclusion on the enigma of Brigham Young there is an idea borrowed from the American National Standards Institute (ANSI) involving testing. Many materials and products require destructive testing. That is, to "prove" performance, the material is destroyed. For example, concrete hardness is measured in compressive strength by putting the material under enough pressure to cause it to break. The point at which it breaks proves the material's hardness. Crash testing of automobiles requires actual collisions. Crash "ratings" are the results of destroying specific car models.

In the Book of Abraham a pre-earth discussion occurs between God, Christ and a council that included Satan. The discussion concerned creating this world and sending all of us here to "prove them herewith, to see if they will do all things whatsoever the Lord their God shall command them[.]"[401] What if we envision that "testing" as necessarily destructive? After all, we are all going to die. If the

---

[400] "But behold, this land, said God, shall be a land of thine inheritance, and the Gentiles shall be blessed upon the land. And this land shall be a land of liberty unto the Gentiles, and there shall be no kings upon the land, who shall raise up unto the Gentiles. And I will fortify this land against all other nations. And he that fighteth against Zion shall perish, saith God. For he that raiseth up a king against me shall perish, for I, the Lord, the king of heaven, will be their king, and I will be a light unto them forever, that hear my words. Wherefore, for this cause, that my covenants may be fulfilled which I have made unto the children of men, that I will do unto them while they are in the flesh, I must needs destroy the secret works of darkness, and of murders, and of abominations." (2 Ne. 10: 10-15.)

[401] Abraham 3: 26; the word "prove" is frequently used in LDS scripture in a similar context: 2 Ne. 11: 3; Ether 12: 35; D&C 98: 12-14; 124: 55; and 132: 51.

process of "proving" involves establishing our limit by the circumstances we find ourselves in, our lives are a revelation to us of what we can do, what we really are, and how we respond to a process that will end, in this phase, with our descent into the grave.

Brigham Young faced greater challenges than we do. We can no more view ourselves living in antebellum America than view ourselves in the shoes of Brigham Young. Therefore, even if we think we understand him, we should hesitate to judge him. That judgment remains best left to God. The most we ought to offer is gratitude we were not given his many tasks to perform, because that test would expose to public view and history's memory our own assortment of human failure.

Governor and President Brigham Young was a colonizer, leader, religious symbol, and American icon. He rightly deserves a place in American and Mormon history, even if some of the praise and criticism given him is both too little and too much.

[POST SCRIPT: An abridgment of this paper was presented at the 2012 Sunstone Symposium. Professor Thomas G. Alexander rebutted the idea of any intention to establish an actual kingship on the part of Governor Young. His criticism has helped to sharpen the focus of this final version. As a result, I added footnotes 231, 245, 248, and 326, as well as a few sentences in this final version.

Brigham Young had himself declared a king before any houses were constructed in 1847. This is now explained in the paper to remove the notion that this was an entirely theoretical idea entertained by Brigham Young. Footnote 231 also clarifies the time frame considered was 1851-58, and acknowledges that, once the anticipated kingdom did not succeed and Brigham Young was removed as Governor, he changed, and the narrative changed.

Brother Alexander's remarks illustrate the anxiety this topic causes, and the desire of many historians to see Brigham Young's remarks in the light of subsequent events, rather than taking them at face value. Readers should be aware of Brother Alexander's criticism, and can listen to his remarks on the Sunstone website. The major criticism he advanced in remarks following the Sunstone presentation was that Brigham Young never self-identified as a "king." That argument is answered in footnote 248, which also references the reader to footnote 245. I am confident that Brother Alexander would not deny the title of prophet to church presidents, even though they do not self-identify with that title. Therefore this criticism proves too much, and is not a reasonable test of Brigham Young's intentions.

Throughout this paper, Brigham Young has been allowed to speak. This, and not Brother Alexander's or my characterization of the man, is the best measure of his heart, as footnote 231 explains.]

THE END